Look I N Me

A Life Shaped by the Most Overlooked

Diane Bailey Nutz

First Edition

ISBN-13: 978-1546646563
ISBN-10:1546646566

Cover design/artwork by: Wynter Designs

Editing: Thank you to Liz and Joan for your ongoing support in perfecting my imperfections, and to Fred and Angel for continual technical support.

DISCLAIMER

Dedicated to my family

and in loving memory of our daughter,

Amy Lynn Nutz (12-1981 to 3-2002)

Dan & Diane Nutz Family 1998

2017 Dan & Diane's Family

With dad Arnold Bailey

CONTENTS

Conclusion

Introduction

Let's Swim!

Raising a child with special needs or becoming disabled yourself is like preparing for a fun dream vacation to La Jolla, California. Imagine that you've made all the preparations in advance by looking up everything about your exciting trip. You've booked a lavish hotel close to the beautiful beach of La Jolla Shores. Part of the anticipation includes looking up sites you want to see and things you will love to do, such as swim, snorkel, walks along the ocean, visit aquariums, museums, shop, and dine in elegant restaurants.

There you are after a long drive arriving at your destination. But instead of seeing the city sign for La Jolla, an Imperial Beach sign glares at you. You are stuck there as your car has broken down and is not repairable. Feeling shocked, your terrific plans have changed. What and where is *Imperial Beach*? You've taken a wrong turn somehow. Booking a hotel not as fancy as the one you had planned leaves you bewildered and confused. There is new and unknown territory to explore and you must figure out how to make this vacation fun and enjoyable. It requires opening your eyes to a whole new world of possibilities. This new place will be dissimilar and more challenging. It may help that it's a smaller city, less affluent and slow paced. There is a beautiful ocean in Imperial Beach as in La Jolla. You will still experience pleasurable, happy and exciting times on this new vacation to Imperial Beach, but they will be unlike your dream vacation plans.

Such life-changing events can happen to any of us at any time. We hope to grow emotionally from such a challenge. The world continues to turn, and we either adjust gracefully or fail miserably.

Look IN Me is about many amazing and courageous individuals and families who have had their vacation plans of going to the beautiful city of La Jolla interrupted with a trip to a not as well-known city of Imperial Beach. Despite unexpected circumstances, they have made the very best of their situation by taking a *swim* despite obstacles.

My life has been greatly enhanced with appreciation for all I've been given. Having spent over half of my life learning of trials beyond my mind's reach, I thank the unique individuals who have been in my life. Appearances may differ, but each person has intrigued and fascinated me as I have worked for or interviewed them as they *swim* through life. These true accounts of the most overlooked are close to my heart. I share them with hope of raising awareness of human beings among us who have been given physical and/or mental challenges. They deserve love, respect, attention and opportunity to progress to their maximum capabilities. As you read of these unique individuals who have shaped my life, may you gain knowledge and feel inspired. And remember to find hilarity along your life's journey. Yes, sometimes, go Nutz!

1

Passionate Beginning

Only God knows my destination of this journey I am on, as it is He who sends me.

Love Them Unconditionally

"Yo go L.A. fly Blue Nangel plane." Diego* is my first memory of meeting an individual with mental disabilities. I was intrigued by him. The next day he truly went to Los Angeles, and flew with the Blue Angels! Whatever he imagined in his head, it would become reality. Who wouldn't want to live life's journey in such a way?

The other side of Diego's life was not as content. People would stare, point, and laugh at his ignorance. He was often misunderstood, left alone and certainly without friends. Back in the 60's and 70's, my father was the operational manager for three separate thrift stores in Southern California. The sign on the store and trucks read, "Profits for the Retarded". I'm sure the R-word was socially and politically accepted back then. Thankfully, Diego didn't understand how demeaning the reference was. He helped in the stores, as part of his educational vocational training. Diego

*Names changed to protect privacy

4

sorted clothing and rags, very much enjoying his rewarding job. His life, though it was imaginary at times, was whatever he made it, which was real to him.

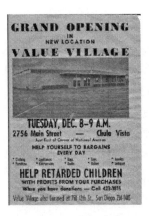

Approximately 1965

And so began my passion toward the individual with special needs. I was taught at an early age through my religion that every human being is a child of God. All are different, but unique and loved by God. Each one of us is treasured; not just the talented, gorgeous, intelligent, rich and so forth. Diversity is what creates uniqueness and acceptance creates unity. I sensed that perhaps people who were intensely unusual were placed on this earth to *teach* the rest of us.

Around age 16, while attending high school, I joined *S Club*. The *S* stood for Service. One of our activities included sitting at a football game with teens that were mentally challenged. At that time they were still referred to as "retarded". They attended their own special high school. These teens were rarely integrated into the rest of the community.

I was assigned to sit with Carol*, who had a tiny head compared to the rest of her body. Her bulging eyes and large ears seemed to absorb the sights and sounds around her. I understood her very well as she spoke to me. She was quite interested in the cheerleaders and enjoyed their chants. When I suggested that perhaps one day she could try out to become a cheerleader, she shrugged and sadly stated, "No, I can never do that. I am retarded." Being quite astonished at her statement, I attempted to give her encouragement. I told her that she should try to be or do anything she wanted in life. Her retort stopped me in my tracks, "My dad says I can't do anything because I'm retarded. I could never be a cheerleader."

Nowadays, thankfully, some things have changed for the better regarding treating all people with dignity and respect. We are not finished with this task however. I've come across many who still use the R-word. They fail to understand that differences can open communication between all human beings and that we *choose* our behaviors. Since love is a verb, *love* can help us to have an open mind and close our eyes to the physical differences.

*Names changed to protect privacy

Diane 1972

Mind-Bending Experience

Once upon a time, the world-renowned mind-reader Samish Imes* was in town to hold a free seminar. Since his record breaking show in London, many of his fans had requested training. Couples everywhere had expressed a desire to learn how to read the mind of their counterpart. Parents were hoping to be educated in the art of figuring out how their teenager came up with such a peculiar scheme. Many thought mind-reading would solve all their problems.

Speculation was that this seminar would be over-booked. Samish prepared a plan of fairness. He would hold this three-hour long class at an odd time. This would weed out those who weren't truly sincere about receiving this exclusive education. The class was scheduled for Monday at 4:00 am.

*fictitious

Samish booked an old choir building with amazing acoustics, which would assist him in teaching the beginners. His experience had taught him the best setting is imperative while bouncing brain waves from one individual to another. The downside of this perfect edifice was that there were only 50 chairs.

There wasn't an abundance of rules for the seminar. You must be an adult and that was about it. Show up to register by 3:30 am, bring a red marker, no paper or electronics allowed as that could interfere with focus and concentration. Being known for his open-mind and non-discrimination, Samish was also famous for his acceptance of others.

The only advertisement Samish had chosen was via fliers. They were plastered all over the city of Phoenix a week before. His promoters didn't understand his way of thinking and Samish always knew this without them saying a word to him. After all, he was the best mind-reader in the world.

Early Monday morning close to 300 potential students patiently awaited their turn to sign-up for the mind-reading class. Unfortunately, only the first 50 would be allowed. This was to their benefit as Samish well knew. It was much easier to concentrate with a smaller crowd. This is an intensely difficult seminar that's packed with technique and instructions.

Noticing a disfigured man in a wheelchair about 12th in line, Samish got concerned. He felt empathy for the man who most likely was totally dependent on others. He must be attending with his guardian who was the most beautiful woman he'd ever seen. He was already sensing impressive brain emissions and intelligence possibly coming from her. Being a lone man for over 56 years weighed heavy on him emotionally. But his career had kept his every waking moment consumed with shows and classes. There was never any time left to date, let alone fall in love and settle down.

The students began to file in. The beautiful woman pushed the disfigured man in the wheelchair toward Samish in the front of the room. She introduced herself as Sheri, and pointing to the man in the wheelchair, said, "This is my brother, Victor, and I will return for him in three hours." His heart could have dropped to the floor as Samish watched her position her brother in the back of the room, and then she vanished.

As instructions began, everyone remembered their red marker. Each student was to place the marker on their desk lengthwise from left to right and focus on it. It impressed the instructor that the man with a severe handicap followed the directions, slowly. The red marker was placed on the tray connected to his wheelchair. Samish doubted Victor could produce brain waves for others to catch or send any out for that matter.

This crowd is half asleep, Samish thought. This will make it easier for me to find those, if any, capable of mind-reading any-thing. It was odd that those who sat in front seemed the most un-aware or proficient at focusing on their teacher. Samish recognized more brain activity toward the mid to back of the classroom.

After the two-hour mark, a test began. "Students, time to stare and focus heavily on the red marker in front of you. Concentrate on the techniques I have taught you. Think of a short sentence that you'd like others to know about you. Make it simple. I like choco-late, or I am strong and so forth." Before the test was completed,

Samish lost *his* focus for a couple of seconds as Sheri returned and sat in the empty seat next to her brother. Victor had been staring at the red marker for practically the entire class. Samish wondered if he was awake.

Everyone was instructed one at a time to tell Samish any sentence they thought they had mind-read from someone else. As he had suspected, not one person got any correct in the front half of the room. Continuing to gradually walk toward the back of the room, he began hearing the same word as a soft murmur from students as they stared at their red marker. "Look." He was hearing the same word in his mind. "Look." He noticed Sheri sat looking confused, but still as lovely as when she had first entered the building. Was this brain length message coming from within her? His eyes met hers. He listened, but no. The message was not coming from Sheri. Her thoughts now were muffled and chaotic since she didn't comprehend what was happening.

Kneeling in front of Victor's wheelchair to be at his eye-level, Samish placed his fingertips of his right hand below Victor's chin and gently raised his face upward. Wow, the voice within Victor was penetrating Samish's mind so clear it was almost deafening. Repeating what Samish *heard,* he spoke the words back to Victor, "Look IN Me." Immediately the young man in the crippled body gave his instructor a quivering grin while a tear streamed down his face. And then another.

The great master mind-reader became the pupil that day. Victor taught him a most important lesson. Despite that Samish was known for his skill and never discriminating, he moved beyond that. From then on Samish would not only attempt to read minds, but to look into the soul as well.

I liken this lesson-learning story to the experiences of the many people with disabilities around the world. They too, yearn to be heard, noticed, given attention and opportunities to progress. Many people have looked right through them and kept walking, not knowing what to say or how to act.

It's been proven to me numerous times that individuals with special needs ache with the same human needs as the rest of the typical populace. They may look different, or not speak, walk, or even feed themselves. Some are completely incapacitated. They too, deserve respect. I perceive these special people would prefer others to look *in* them, instead of looking *at* them.

Thirty Plus Years

I was in my late 20's, going through a divorce after almost 13 years of marriage. I had fought to avoid statistics, which stated, 90 percent of those who marry in their teens end up divorced. We had joined the 90 percent club. My major concern was for my four young children, and my emotional and monetary adjustments. Up to this time, I'd held only part-time work, at babysitting and teaching macramé. Forced into the work force to survive, I went to the school district hoping to find a job with the same hours as my three school-aged children.

Bingo! And so it began. ...

I skipped around for a while that first year, supervising in the cafeteria, doing clerical work, working as a nurse's aide and an instructional aide for the special needs classroom. Being a substitute was the answer to my earning a paycheck.

If my children were sick, I wouldn't accept an assignment. The sitter of my one-year-old was a sweet, loving lady who only watched two children in her home, and her home-cooked, Thai meals were a perk for my youngest.

The first time I received a call inquiring if I would work with special needs kids, I said, "Sure, why not!"

The line went silent for a few seconds. "You'll do it?"

My background came into play, as you can see, in my favor. I began to get only those types of substitute assignments. Most were for mentally and physically disabled individuals, the majority were quite severe. My heart went out to them, most disabled since birth. This type of job took a lot of hardcore strength, patience, compassion and good health.

Their teachers, (I call them "the Saints") with teaching credentials in hand and wearing their hearts on their sleeves, gave children with very little potential a chance. A chance to succeed at something. Anything! I was amazed at these wonderful mentors with patience never ending, and filled with genuine love. It would benefit all mankind if we each would sit in a classroom and observe this setting. My blessings in life became more alive and vast.

Some drawbacks I became aware of in this profession were mostly physical. I stood in often for those teachers who were on medical leave due to an injury of the back, shoulder, or knee. I was astonished that the staff could eat lunch around these *children* who drooled and at times looked and smelled as if they needed a good long scrubbing in the tub. There probably was not the proper number of caregivers needed for their hygiene needs. Unable to stomach the smell, I would sit and eat my lunch in my car. I even felt guilty about that.

There was a group home located in the school district for the severely mentally and physically disabled ages six to 21 years old. They were housed overnight and cared for by nurses and caregivers. Monday through Friday, caregivers loaded the children into wheelchairs. Their special school was across the parking lot, where certified teachers *taught* them. Most of these unique individuals had to be lifted, bathed, fed, and diapered. Some were already full-grown adults of course, since they lived there through age 21.

The six large classrooms were anything but typical. Mats and cots covered the floors, and portable toilets hid behind barriers for a minority of the students able to use them. There were a few gigantic hammock-type swings. Only one student could speak. Charlie* was quite popular with the staff, being able to request some needs and even laugh.

The school encouraged the families of these special people to visit, but I rarely saw visitors there. Hopefully, parents came to visit their children after school hours. But I was told that was uncommon. I truly believe these special folks would benefit from regular family visits.

I fell in love with little Paul*, only six years old, and such a gorgeous child. He was blind, deaf and physically unable to move. At age two, Paul had contracted a high fever and suffered a seizure which took all his abilities and life potential away. I

*Names changed to protect privacy

couldn't imagine the throbbing heartfelt pain his parents must have felt. His father visited about every other day, and I saw recognition from an otherwise lifeless child.

Watching Paul and his father interact supported my belief of the need for human contact. His father held him, talked to him as he touched his face and caressed Paul's limbs, and combed his long dark hair. When Paul's father placed ear phones over his ears and played extremely loud classical music, Paul smiled. Either he wasn't completely deaf, or he felt vibrations. Or, he felt love is the best therapy.

Going home to my four healthy children was the best therapy I had after a long workday. I realized more, after being part of a different world, that there are many problems that could arise at birth and after. Thinking of all the healthy births that cross the threshold every day is astounding. Until being surrounded by children with disabilities, I admit, I had taken it somewhat for granted that my babies were born healthy.

This school/care center I've talked about wasn't in the school educational system very long. It became too costly to justify certified teachers being paid to give the lowliest of children opportunity to succeed. If it meant turning their head to look at a light, or blinking on cue, I suppose members in society thought it not important enough. I saw the reward however, mostly in the teachers' faces. The persistence the teachers encompassed was of value to those dear, unique *children*.

Not the Jolly Green Giant

It was late 1980. A vivid memory stands out in my mind. At age 27, I was a happy and busy mother of four children who ranged from infancy to age seven. I didn't have a problem traveling with all of my children. No matter where we went, there was much to learn. And that included me.

Whatever the destination, we'd hear from at least one person, "Are they all yours?" I felt a sense of love and pride to answer, "Sure are and lovin it!" It's a shame they didn't catch a glimpse of me years later when those numbers doubled.

I was confident I had taught my older children social correctness. We'd discuss differences in appearance such as folks with missing limbs, peculiar faces, different skin tones, those in wheelchairs, and the blind. I even explained to my children that not every large woman is pregnant. I thought I had covered all the bases, until we happened to go to the grocery store one afternoon.

I began, as usual, selecting groceries from my long list, aisle by aisle. My baby girl sat in the cart's seat with a stretchy belt around her waist for safety (my own invention). The others took turns helping to pick things out, or fetching items off the shelves.

And then, from the corner of my eye, I saw her, a little person! Back then, it was still acceptable to call them midgets. Wow, I had not covered this with my children.

I tried to avoid the woman because I didn't want the children asking questions. My trek through the grocery store became noticeably strange to my two oldest offspring, Rochelle and Freddie. They kept informing me we were going the wrong way or that we'd already been down this aisle two times. Finally, I believed the little woman had finished and had left the building. After all, how much could she stack in the small handled basket she'd carried?

Whew! We finally got in line to check out. Only three shoppers were in front of us. The lines were unusually long for a weekday afternoon. I was sorting through my coupons when I heard Freddie exclaim, "Look Mom, I'm taller than her!"

Wouldn't you know it; the little woman had the audacity to stroll around the store unnecessarily for the sole purpose of positioning herself behind the woman with four inquisitive children.

Trying to redirect my seven-year-old son was next to impossible, as he delighted in suddenly becoming a giant. I proceeded to teach him, though, a bit late, that people come in all sizes. Short people can be even smarter than tall people and on and on. "But Mom! Why is she so short? Look, I am way taller!" He was motioning with his hand to give me the play-by-play account from the top of his head angling downward to the top of hers, over and over again, as if she were an inanimate object.

Embarrassed, I apologized to the elderly woman, as she was probably in her 40's. (My perspective on age has changed since then.) It was to no avail, as she gave us—a flustered mother and an over-the-top gleeful child—an angry, bug-eyed stare. I expected her to be more understanding. She uttered nothing. Perhaps this was the straw that broke the camel's back; this had happened one too many times.

I made sure my children took their place in front of the cart, as I loaded groceries on to the conveyer belt. The conveyor belt of groceries that day seemed unending, more so than usual. Of course, after this experience, I realized I still had many learning experiences ahead of me as I took my children grocery shopping with me.

Thankful to be in the car, with all occupants safely secured, I ripped open the newly purchased extra-large bag of Peanut M&M's. I pulled on to the main road as the children and I chowed down on handfuls of the consoling candy. M&M's never tasted so delicious!

Influential Memories

If I were to analyze my beginnings under a magnifying glass, I would say that my mother was the largest influence in my life. Oft times, without the realization, quiet minutes of our life turn us into better people.

As I was writing this book, my mother's silent power almost went unrecognized. Her example of sweetness radiated from her inner essence. She was genuinely and consistently caring to those in need. There was never a time where she wasn't serving her husband, showing unwavering love. When I was in my teens, I thought on one occasion, "My dad sure didn't deserve her carting his dinner to that TV tray tonight! He just yelled at me because I was with friends he didn't approve of, which isn't a big deal. She's still catering to his every need. I don't get it!"

I doubt there was a mean bone in her body. My mother was one of the most social people I've ever known. She could walk into a grocery store to purchase a few items and come out two hours later having met at least seven new life-long friends. And believe me, they knew her life story as well, and especially how she idealized her husband, my father.

Don't think that I'm trying to paint a picture that my mother was perfect. She insisted once that I needed to be spanked. I had accidentally (honest) dropped a large toy on my little brother Arnold Jr.'s head. We all knew that he was her favorite. My mother took out her cloth belt and attempted to spank me with it. I think she was hurting a lot more than I was, trying to hold me over her lap as I wiggled and squirmed.

After I had my own children, I realized what my mother felt having a family she loved. There's a sense of pride and great reward raising children.

I was taught from an early age to treat everyone with respect and kindness. Finally, I am feeling grateful for being shown what selfless service is. It's about time I recognized my angel mother's influence in my choice of careers, caring for others.

Hindsight gives us regrets at times. I believe I told my mother thank you for modeling sweetness, but I'm not sure. If I could see her in person, I would tell her again and with more depth of sincere appreciation. I will have to wait for that chance. My mother, Lena, went on ahead of the rest of her family in June 2008.

Photo provided by Paul Norris

Bailey Family 1984

Arnold Jr., Diane, Mom Lena, Dad Arnold, Monica, Randy

2

My Unscripted Education

Surprises along the way teach me life's grandest lessons.

Danger!

Upon moving to Arizona, I found myself job hunting again. I was yet asked the same question, "Will you work with special needs?" "Yes (duh)." Landing a job is easy with that answer. Being an avid health nut(z) and working out or staying fit by skating, or playing soccer and other games with my children, I knew I was in shape to take on a physically demanding job.

But "E.H. children"? What was that?

Emotionally handicapped, what an eye-opener. I was placed in a junior high and only had to teach and be responsible for one student. I wondered how this assignment could be that tricky. Johnny* was bigger than me in every way. I saw how he bothered the teacher and aide. Johnny knew how to scare them by positioning himself in their personal space. Nervously, they'd step back. He was best known for throwing chairs. Having eight children, I was not easily intimidated.

*Names changed to protect privacy

24

Since Johnny's attention span was shorter than an ant, my assignment was to sit with him in an empty classroom when he had a writing assignment. He and I got along wonderfully. He didn't have a father in the home and perhaps he didn't even know who his sperm donor was. I got the picture soon enough though. This mother felt sorry for her son and would believe him if he said school's closed for a snow day. Come on. In Phoenix, Arizona?

There was always that chance I would need to take a day off, not for vacation mind you, but for a sick child. It happens now and then with our numbers. I was only gone one day, but got an earful on my return. The substitute took Johnny to the usual empty class-room and something went wrong. Chairs started to fly and Johnny was immediately locked in the room, alone, until the principal could take over for the substitute. Wow, I had missed it! It would have been more exhilarating to see airborne chairs than getting meds for my son's monthly ear infections. Poor Johnny had to stay home with his doting, but foolish mother for a two-day suspension. Was that a suitable consequence?

We had in this same E.H. classroom a much more dangerous student. Unlike Johnny, who looked very typical, Mason* was al-most round from head to toe, with bright, little eyes. He had ag-gressive tendencies, to say the least. No one — and I mean NO ONE — was allowed to stand within arm's reach of him. It was a rule that everyone had to remember and obey at all times, or Mason might cause harm and be ousted to the time-out partition. His aide, Lindsey*, was younger and much smaller than I

*Names changed to protect privacy

was. Being physically and mentally strong, Lindsey was a top notch choice for Mason's one-on-one aide. I had two days of training with her and Mason while Johnny was expelled, so that I could substitute for Lindsey in case she was ever absent.

Mason's favorite aggressive outburst was to pull glasses off the closest face and snap them in half. His short arms and tiny hands were faster than the Road Runner escaping from the Coyote! Oops, the teacher leaned over Mason to explain an assignment, a bit too close! That was her second pair of glasses wrecked beyond repair in only four months. Off he went to the time-out chair behind the partition. Mason was not a happy camper.

Within minutes I heard splashing water come from behind the partition. Could it be? Oh my, yes. Mason found it a great form of rebellion to urinate on the carpet in front of the chair he sat on. With Lindsey being absent, I had the honor of walking him to the principal's office, observing the cardinal rule of staying beyond arm's reach.

I learned some facts about Mason's family and home life. He had two younger siblings who had to be protected from their big brother. His parents worked diligently to keep peace and safety in the home. Mason had the remodeled basement to himself. He loved game time on his computer, but coming home early from school meant his gaming privilege was lost. I later heard that once, while his mother was driving him home, Mason took his seatbelt off and started swinging his fists wildly at her. Perhaps she had grown accustomed to his behaviors. It amazes me how patient most parents of children with special needs are.

Find Room to Laugh

After managing to survive two years in the junior high realm, I welcomed a new assignment with glee at an elementary school in the Tempe school district, working with students shorter than myself. Another plus was that my five-year-old daughter Nikki got a boundary exception to attend all-day kindergarten at the school. Traveling to and from work with her was one of the best perks a job could offer.

I was introduced to the teacher, Mrs. Posh*, and assistant, Beverly*, in the new classroom with mentally and some physically disabled students, ages eight to 12 years. These two ladies had an air of enthusiasm about them I had never experienced in my 11 years in the field. Most teachers' energy levels seemed drained; they often gave off a tired appearance.

We had nine students, giving us a three-to-one ratio. Most students were ambulatory, and had a very low I.Q. (under 70). Only two students, including Mario*, were verbal. The students were

*Names changed to protect privacy

taught to call their instructors by their last name, so I was Mrs. Nutz. Mario was a curious type of boy, average in that aspect, and often asked me what my first name was. I kept him in the dark about it, for a while.

My husband, Dan, had an opportunity to substitute teach in my classroom. Mario overheard Dan quietly speaking to me. He then exclaimed, "I know your first name, Mrs. Nutz! It's HONEY! I heard Mr. Nutz call you that!" Because of Mario, I became the *Honey Nutz*.

Toothful Wonder

The pupils in our classroom were encouraged to interact with other students in such places as the cafeteria and recess. This encouraged proper behavior, modeled by their peers, most of the time. If our students misbehaved, we would have them sit out recess on the side, with one of us supervising.

On one occasion Alfred* was sitting out his recess. This was his consequence for swinging his arms vigorously, hitting students passing by. Alfred had a tracheotomy and was unable to speak. I was the fortunate adult assigned to sit near Alfred that day. As I observed Alfred, while he sat on the sidewalk, he kept inserting his fingers into his mouth, which was something new for him. Being intrigued, I watched him for a few more minutes. Then, there it was, a tooth, clinched in his right fist!

*Names changed to protect privacy

I placed Alfred's tooth in a paper towel and brought it to the classroom after recess. Mrs. Posh sent Alfred and his tooth, with Beverly's assistance, to the nurse's office to verify which tooth he had lost, and write a note home to Alfred's mother. Beverly could hardly stop laughing long enough to catch her breath upon their return. The tooth Alfred had pulled out of his mouth was NOT his!

We wondered if the Tooth Fairy would be perplexed. To think, somewhere out on the playground, a student, other than Alfred, had really lost a tooth and would be overlooked by the Tooth Fairy!

Panic State to Career Choice

Imagine your worst fears often coming to life. Poor Juan* was scared to death of the dark and loud noises. We instructed the staff, after prior experiences, to notify us before practice fire drills. Perhaps different staff members took turns at the drills and never got the memo, because we continued to be caught off-guard. And once again, the startling shrill alarm would occur. Before we had time to react, Juan would run out the door! He was unable to escape the torturous sound, since the noise was transmitted inside and outside of classrooms. It took quite a few minutes to calm Juan down and assure him the awful loud monster was dead, once more.

For Juan's well-being, the dark was something we could usually control. However, taking our students to an all-school assembly was taking a chance because we would not have control of the lighting. As quick as you could snap your fingers, the lights were turned off to show a video and then he was off—roly-poly Juan— out the door. Panic was in his chubby little face every time this

*Names changed to protect privacy

happened, and I felt empathy for him. I imagined it would be like someone lining up my children at the edge of the Grand Canyon with no barriers. Terror would fill my body and soul.

Meeting the students' parents was always an experience, and each a diverse encounter. I didn't envy their challenge of raising such unique individuals. I had enough trials of my own with my amazing biological and step-children. Working with this different population gave me gratitude for my own blessings that I couldn't have gained at any other job.

A parent I came to know well, and who turned me to a new aspect in my career, was Mark's* mother, Denise*. Mark was her fifth child; he had been born with autism. Denise was a nurse by profession and had known early on something was not right with her baby.

Mark looked like any other boy of eight years, and to top off matters, he was a handsome young man. By age eight, Mark had learned to speak. However, most of Mark's words were repetitive. His parents and teachers were consistent in teaching him to verbalize his needs, instead of merely copying those around him. This mother and father needed some extra help with their son, Mark.

When Denise asked if I had ever thought of doing respite in my home, I had to ask her to explain what that was exactly. She explained that most caregivers of people with disabilities are allowed

---

*Names changed to protect privacy

monthly respite (or reprieve) hours, paid by the state. The respite worker attends several classes to become certified for the job and obtains a fingerprint card. This sparked an interest in me.

After completing a few required classes, becoming certified and obtaining fingerprint clearance with the State of Arizona, I became a certified caregiver, respite, attendant care, and habilitation provider. Proper insurance and a car inspection were also required for times I would need to transport the individuals. After a home inspection, a few modifications completed the licensing process.

I've often thought, in hindsight, I should have thanked Denise for enlightening me with a new job opportunity. Respite and caregiving became my niche in the workforce. I found a new passion because of the many inspiring parents I met while caring for their children with special needs.

Ice Cream, Anyone?

My first respite clients were Mark and Denny*, from the elementary school classroom. When requested, after school, I would simply drive them to my home and care for them, giving the parent(s) a reprieve. Other than helping with our finances, this became a learning opportunity for my own children. They gained understanding and acceptance of those with differences. I could also see that it helped them become less self-centered.

I was privileged to work with Mark through his teen years. As time passed and Mark matured, he became even more attractive. One morning, I drove my youngest daughter, Nikki, to a high school fund raiser car wash for her cheer squad. Mark came along with us. One of Nikki's friends said she hoped to meet her hot brother who was in the car. This gave us all a good laugh and embarrassed the friend. Mark didn't comprehend such compliments.

*Names changed to protect privacy

Another time, I took Mark and some other children to the public library. This location was a safe place for Mark, with supervision, since he was usually a very silent teenager. Three female adolescents slowly approached him, saying, "Hi," with friendly smiles. He politely showed off a gorgeous grin. The girls walked away giggling, completely clueless.

There were times when I would have welcomed verbalization from Mark, especially on this day. The park activity seemed perfectly planned. Feeling optimistic, with six children safely secured in my van, we headed toward Treatsville, McDonald's, you know, for ice cream cones. What better manner to begin our outing? My two youngest children invited friends to join in the fun. Mark and another teenager with special needs, Jack*, were also with us.

I ordered outside at the drive-through speaker, four chocolate, and three vanilla cones. As I began to pull forward to pay, I heard and felt a splatter on the back of my seat. At that exact moment, most occupants behind me yelled out, "EWWWW, GROSS!"

You probably guessed that Mark was sick and seated directly behind me. No warning, no verbalizing had proceeded from his mouth before the regurgitation. I couldn't pull up to the pick-up window, pay for, and receive the ice cream cones quickly enough. I handed cones and napkins to the children, well, all but Mark. I wondered if his three huge heaves had emptied him.

*Names changed to protect privacy

To be expected, most of us had lost our appetite for even a delectable, cooling ice cream cone. My children asked if they *had* to eat their cones. As I drove home, explaining that the destination to the park would have to wait, I could only manage to keep my cone from melting down my hand with an occasional slurp.

Looking in my rear view mirror, I spotted Jack with three cones balanced in his large hands, happily licking away. My son, Speedy, who had been seated next to Mark, had changed seats with Jack, after Mark's unexpected outburst. Apparently, Jack had a cast iron stomach and was oblivious to the smell and sight of vomit. I'm not sure, but I believe Jack enjoyed a few more ice cream cones after we returned home.

A Just Reward of Training

This unusually warm afternoon was my turn to supervise our students in the cafeteria. It never failed that Denny was the very last student to be finished with his lunch. That's correct. Out of all the students in that elementary school, he was always the grand finale to depart from the lunch room.

Chewing very slowly was routine for Denny. I sat near him on the bench observing and encouraging him. Usually, he insisted on finishing every single bite. Since the recess hadn't ended, we sat patiently in the air-conditioned cafeteria.

I noticed even the three cafeteria workers were in the back doing dishes and cleaning up. No one was in sight. I was beginning to be really bored as I watched the hands on the clock moving ever so slowly.

This was several years ago before cameras were installed in the schools in some areas. Denny had almost finished his lunch, when he began gagging. I told him to cough it out. Then I yelled for him to keep trying to cough. It was to no avail. I didn't panic, but thought to myself, time to kick-start my training knowledge. Now!

Placing my hands together in a fist in the center below his ribcage, I began thrusting inward and upward. On the third quick movement, out flew a wad of chewed up celery! Oh wow, abdominal thrusts really work!

As we exited the cafeteria, the custodian was coming in to clean up the tables and floors. I mentioned to him in passing what had just happened. We both agreed, no more celery for Denny!

The recess bell sounded before Denny could make his way to the playground. My heart was still in hyper mode, but my pal, Denny, was as slow moving and calm as ever. The excitement hadn't fazed him in the least.

A note was sent home to his grandmother about the almost tragic situation. Rules of supervision for these unique students seemed even more important now, as well as the training needed to handle these types of emergencies.

Movie Time Fun

On some occasions, I have really leaned into the name, Nutz. You sink or swim with a name like that. Dan learned early on to *swim* with his last name. We had a large family, so some would think us a bit crazy. But I totally loved the amusement created by the diversity of each family member. There's always excitement, be it good or bad. Never a dull moment. We do believe that humor can be the best medicine.

Other times, when we added children with special needs to our clan, we, even more so experienced "Going Nutz". It was helpful when my husband, Dan, was free to accompany me on exhilarating activities with the children. Taking several children to an inexpensive movie usually kept them entertained. With Dan there, I was at ease about the boys with special needs using the restroom. Usually, I would ask my son, Speedy, to check on them and give those verbal prompts if needed, such as, "Turn off the water," "Pull your pants up," "Let's go," and "Quit splashing in that!"

Fortunately, Dan was with us when Jack and Mark might have to use the facilities. I never would have heard the full description without him there. The movie was over and the men headed to *their* place to relieve themselves. Mark and Jack proceeded to the urinals and dropped their pants, all the way to the floor. One hairy backside, one not, stood out to every male within eye-shot. Every time someone stared at the grown men with pants on the floor, Dan would have to explain, "Don't worry. They're with me."

For the Love of Cheeks!

Children on the autism spectrum usually develop obsessive routines and more routines on top of that. Mark was living proof of this. Supervising him called for a great deal of staying power at times. Walking to the car sometimes required waiting while he circled the inside borders of my garage three times. Washing his hands often took four tries before he knew he was finished. Seems like nonsense to most of us, but with Mark and many others with autism, it is their way of life.

I took Mark with me one afternoon to pick up my van from the repair shop. My oldest daughter, Rochelle, dropped us off at the dealer, knowing my car was ready. I would only be required to make payment and retrieve my keys. Homeward bound we would go. This proved much more difficult and exasperating than expected.

Before I could pull my checkbook out, Mark had decided he needed to lightly touch the side of my face. Displaying his wide handsome grin, Mark whispered, "Cheeks, cheeks," softly touching my face with his index finger. After three times of this cheeks touching routine, I instructed him, "Mark, please sit over there and we'll leave soon." I had almost finished writing the check when an elderly gentleman (perhaps in his 70's), who had apparently entered the room a few steps behind us, approached me with a huge scowl on his face.

Getting in my space, the man asked if that young man over there was with me. I glanced over my shoulder and saw that the man and his young-looking (about mid 30's), dirty, and raggedly dressed wife had sat right next to Mark; even though it looked like at least 15 empty chairs remained elsewhere. There was Mark, grinning from ear to ear.

This man was so angry I thought he may spit nails at my face. He exclaimed, "That young man is touching my wife's cheeks and I'm going to call the police on him!"

"Oops," I told him. He repeated his threat. I tried, to no avail, to describe the special need's attributes of autism that Mark possessed. I knew if I would have let Mark finish his routine, however many times that would have been, of touching *my* cheeks, this man would not be complaining about his wife being molested. The woman remained quiet, in her seat, staring straight ahead. Mark continued looking at her with his amazing smile.

I sped up my check writing and assured the man we were leaving. I continued trying to convince him that Mark was perfectly innocent of any illicit behaviors. The easily agitated man firmly stated that he did not care if Mark had any special problems, and that nobody touches his wife! I paid, snatched up my keys, and instructed Mark to apologize to the nice lady. He continued his beaming smile and softly said, "Sorry?"

As we were leaving, Mark was still saying to me, "Nice cheeks, nice cheeks." From her appearance, that was a very nice compliment for Mark to give this woman. However, her husband was anything but nice to Mark.

Denise, Mark's mother, told me this type of incident happened often. Most people were not considerate or tolerable of his disability. Many would not believe he had autism because of his striking appearance. I admit I had it easy raising children with the typical behaviors that seemed difficult enough for me to handle at times. Thank goodness none of our children possessed a love of cheeks!

Master Informer

On some occasions, I drove Denny to my home after school to stay until his grandmother returned from work. Denny and his sister were born with fetal alcohol syndrome. Their mother cared for his sister and grandma was guardian to Denny. Both children were ambulatory but unable to speak any intelligible words. Grandmothers, such as Denny's, are my heroes.

Most would be amazed at Denny's individual *vocabulary*. He communicated better than other children his age, by using hand signals and expressive tones. Other times, his body language said it all.

On one such occasion, I had made a quick escape to the bathroom. I figured at least one child would come knocking on the door before I could finish up my business. Other mothers know this to be the norm. The knocking began, along with loud mumbling. Denny was alerting me to something of importance. I hurried out, Denny immediately grabbing my hand and pulling me to the living room. He was almost to the going-to-pieces stage as he frantically pointed to Jack. I didn't have to say a word because Jack jerked his hand out of our fish aquarium, obviously fully aware of his wrongdoing. Thankfully, all fish were accounted for. I hoped Jack wasn't acquiring a taste for sushi. He needed to stick to munching down on several ice cream cones (*Ice Cream, Anyone?*) per sitting.

My own children couldn't hold a candle to Denny, our master informant. Who needs the English language to communicate, when you have your very own dialect anyone can understand?

3

Need for Inclusion

Disabled <Imperfect> Everyone

Just Ask Me

The Simmons* family had a son and a daughter. The parents were quite hesitant to bring Richard* to my house without knowing our family. I understood completely, as Richard was an intelligent 14-year-old. However, he had no voice of his own, having been afflicted with cerebral palsy at birth. He was confined to a wheelchair and found it difficult at times to communicate his needs. The mother asked if the older daughter, Jasmine*, could come to assist me on his first visit. I welcomed her help.

At this time we had six children of our own living at home. It was never boring in the Nutz home with so many different personalities. It was apparent from the start that Richard thrived on all the activity. I loved hearing his enthusiastic laughter. Jasmine got along nicely with our family. I think she may have been disappointed that she would only get one visit with us, but one visit was what the parents had hoped for.

*Names changed to protect privacy

A few months after Richard became a regular visitor in our home, the Arizona Department of Developmental Disabilities equipped him with a communication device. It was rectangular and about nine inches by eight inches, mounted in an upright position on Richard's wheelchair tray. The device had approximately 30 different boxes representing things Richard may need to communicate to others. The most difficult chore for Richard was to touch the correct box. Having cerebral palsy made this seemingly easy task a complex challenge for him. However, he worked at it diligently. Richard was persistent, always.

A few of the things Richard would convey to us with the female voice on his device were: "I need to use the restroom." "Can I go outside?" and "I'm hungry." Also, he had a list of foods he enjoyed. He had an array of things important in his life as well, such as the names of his loved ones, where he went to school, teachers, favorite activities, music, and movie titles programmed into his device. I would encourage visitors to carry on a conversation with Richard. They were very impressed, and Richard could feel a bit typical as well as valued.

I had been asked to teach a lesson entitled "Accepting All as Children of God" to the women's group in our church. The article I was to use discussed many social aspects such as cultures, race, experiences in backgrounds, and appearances, but nowhere did it speak of people with special needs. Whoa, here was my chance to share!

Being a tactile person at heart, I searched for hands-on experiences and visual examples. Richard's mother agreed to wheel him into the classroom at the designated time. Richard was 17 years old now and had great control of his electronic wheelchair. I had 35 minutes to teach and was ready for Richard to come to the front of the room when 15 minutes remained. He proudly maneuvered his motorized wheelchair front and center.

I asked Richard to introduce himself and he did so, via his communication device, slowly but accurately. He told the ladies (through the female voice on his machine) his name, school, parents' and sister's names. Then I instructed the group to ask Richard something else about himself. Silence. Dead silence. I noticed Richard's smiling enthusiasm had faded.

Finally, my friend, Gail*, who had adopted Adam*, a baby with Down syndrome, two years previously, raised her hand and asked Richard about his favorite food. She continued conversing with him for a few minutes because not one lady would join in. With my encouragement, a few more hesitantly inquired further about Richard's likes and dislikes. I sensed his mood cheered up.

As my lesson concluded, I felt a bit disappointed as the ladies were so hesitant to converse with Richard. It seemed I was not able to transmit my passion for people with special needs to the ladies. I was grateful that Gail was quite willing to carry on a conversation with Richard comfortably and had broken the ice in the room. Later she thanked me for that concrete real-life example integrating a special person into our group. As it turned out, several gals had come up to Gail's little boy born with challenges and spoke to him after class. They normally wouldn't have even acknowledged his presence. Sweet success.

*Names changed to protect privacy

Mighty

The Moore* family adopted little Adam when he was two years old. Adam was a loveable child with Down syndrome. This family had three older children as well, and another daughter born when Adam was seven years old. The entire family fell in love with this special child born with gorgeous green eyes and a killer smile. With Adam joining their family, the strong bond of love they shared increased.

When Adam was three years old, he was still quite tiny and unable to walk. If you saw him then, you'd have guessed he was about one year old. His mother carried him everywhere. But sometimes Adam would have a notion to be held by others and would lunge forward, reaching his arms out.

His mother, Gail, related an incident to me that humbled her when she made a hurried stop at a grocery store. She was hastening her steps leaving the store, when she spotted a rough-looking man,

*Names changed to protect privacy

dirty, with a spiked collar, and reeking of alcohol. She had to stop in her tracks as little Adam immediately lunged and held his arms out to the man. At first the man tried to ignore the small child. He finally mumbled, "Hey, buddy." Adam was quite insistent this man hold him. He was not judging the person on his appearance, and his mother realized she would be setting a poor example if she were to do so. Smiling, she encouraged the guy to hold her son. They exchanged conversation for a few minutes. It was noticeable Adam had cheered up this stranger. But to Adam, this man was no stranger.

Later that year, when the Moores' daughter was dressing for baptism at their Latter-day Saints (Mormon) church, she needed her mother's assistance with her clothing and combing her hair. It had been a short time since the finalization of Adam's adoption, and he was very attached to his new mommy. There were many in attendance who offered to hold and entertain the little guy while his mother helped her daughter. Adam was not willing to be held by his father, or anyone else, but instead lunged with outstretched arms to his grandmother.

Mrs. Moore hesitated to let him go because this woman had been very uncomfortable with and unsupportive of Adam's adoption. But unable to keep him from jumping into his grandmother's lap, she allowed him to go. Her mother-in-law nodded her approval. At first she did not hold him close. It was very noticeable this woman was not at ease holding Adam.

As the baptism continued, Adam was happily sitting in his grandmother's lap. The woman became more relaxed as time went on. She gradually held Adam lovingly and was charmed by his adoring affection. A few offered to take him, but she quickly denied them the honor. Adam won his grandmother's heart that day independent of others' previous attempts to help.

Photo provided by Gail

The Church of Jesus Christ of Latter-day Saints is divided into areas called wards. The different wards are assigned various meeting times. Often, it becomes necessary to divide these wards as neighborhoods change. The church has young men and young women classes for their youth. When the Moores' ward boundaries were reorganized, Adam was around 15 years old.

The young men's group for ages 12 to18 was much larger in numbers than previously. Adam had been with five other young men before the division. Now there were a total of 25, so only a few knew Adam. They meet on Sundays as well as during the week. There were two or three adult leaders. One of them told the boys they were going to have a pull-up contest. He gave them a challenge that they would add up the total number of pull-ups the boys could do, and then one of the leaders would match that number. If the boys won, the leaders would take them for a treat. The boys accepted the challenge wholeheartedly.

They found a chin-up bar at a nearby park and the contest began. Some of the boys could only muster one or two pull-ups. Some weren't able to accomplish a single one with proper form. To their disappointment, the boys achieved only 25 total pull-ups. A leader happily did the 25, adding a 26th for good measure.

But then one of the boys brought to everyone's attention that Adam didn't get a turn. Most had assumed that he wouldn't be able to execute a pull-up. Wrong! When he stepped up to the bar, Adam could not only do a pull-up, but he beat them all. He did a total of 27! The leader was spent and not able to do one more pull-up. Off the group went for ice cream, thanks to Adam. Never again did any of them take for granted what Adam could or could not do. A disability diagnoses does not describe aptitudes.

Playtime Please

Much in society has progressed in a positive aspect in the past 30 years to help people with disabilities, including children with special needs. They are out and about in the public and integrated into public schools. Special Olympics is very successful in giving children and adults who are unable to participate in regular sports a chance to compete, and an opportunity to experience triumphs and friendships with rewarding activities.

However, there still are those children with special needs, where being an active participant means only sitting and observing. They are unable to run, walk, throw a ball, skate, slide, swing, play a video game, participate in any sport or create an art project or even speak. If an individual is extremely mentally and physically disabled, they still have typical human needs and desires.

Over the years, I've taken care of individuals with varying degrees of disabilities, but have become aware they don't differ that much from the rest of us. If you pay attention to the body language or sounds these unique people display, sometimes you discover by trial and error what it is they are trying to communicate. And that is a great accomplishment as well as a fulfilling moment.

I came to realize that Richard enjoyed watching the other children play in my backyard—running, swinging, sliding, and throwing balls. I asked Richard if he had ever been on a slide. His eyes widened, virtually shaping into a scary glare. At the time, it was still reasonable for me to lift Richard with no harm to him, or to my back. He was stiff, which made the task a bit awkward. I lifted him gently and slowly. (I was careful enough to know ahead of time whether I should attempt this feat.) Laying him down in the middle of the slide, I let him glide to the bottom of the slide while I held one of his hands. His laughter was magical!

On another occasion, when we were moving rocks into our backyard, I got the brilliant idea to give Richard a ride in the wheelbarrow. I was almost 100 percent sure he had never had that thrill. I admit he seemed wary of the opportunity, but once I started to run with him in the wheel barrow, I knew he didn't want this ride to ever end. Back and forth across my yard I sprinted. After a few laps, my sprinting slowed to a walk. Richard kept encouraging me with his loud giggles. Talk about a good work out for me. Most of all, my reward was priceless.

Ba-nan-a!

Andrea was so tiny; my children asked me if she was a munchkin in *The Wonderful Wizard of Oz.* Her short body was pudgy, and her misshaped mouth made it difficult for her to swallow or speak properly. Fortunately for her, and to the laughter of others, she could slowly shout out one intelligible word in her hoarse little voice, "Ba-nan-a!" My children would about split a gut hearing her articulate that one and only audible word.

Andrea moved slowly and tired easily. When she was in the mood, she wore hearing aids and was decent at sign language. She had frequent bladder infections and bronchitis. But Andrea loved to laugh and was full of spunk and mischief.

When I began providing respite for Andrea, she was 11 years old. She enjoyed watching quirky movies. She preferred to sneak up quietly and sit on the couch, behind Nikki or Speedy, my two youngest. She would go unnoticed until her teeny fingers intertwined through the hair of one of them. Then she'd yank, and they'd yell! I'd remind Nikki and Speedy not to sit in front of Andrea. They'd let me know that they were on the floor first.

Sneaky, little Andrea pulled this ploy often. It wasn't easy for me to untwist the hair tangled around her tiny fingers. She did know how to transform my children's screams into smiles though: "Ba-nan-a!"

Going to the man-made lake near their home with her father was one of Andrea's cherished pastimes. The ducks knew them well, as Andrea always tossed bread crumbs their way. She was still daddy's little girl, even into her 20's and early 30's. By then, her two siblings were married and raising their own children.

Imagine one of your children without the physical or mental capability to mature into an adult. This may sound delightful at first. How would you welcome your baby staying young, cuddling, never growing up and making adult decisions? The down-side to this might be: unending diapers, ongoing feedings, constant super-vision and assisting. The child would always be your baby, no matter how large they grew bodily.

I've lost track of most of the children with special needs whom I've cared for over 30 years, through moves and life changes. Three weeks after Andrea's life on earth came to an end was when I received the heartbreaking news. She was 31 years old. Her mother and father were devastated by the loss of their baby girl. Their lives had revolved around Andrea's care, and they felt a huge void. My husband, Dan, and I visited with them in their home, shortly after Andrea's passing. We felt great empathy for them. Having lost a daughter at age 20 in an accident several years earlier, we could relate somewhat with what they were going through. Andrea's parents continue to deeply feel her absence, but they sense their angel daughter's presence often. Here's to Andrea, "Ba-nan-a!" We miss you!

From Andrea's mother:

Andrea had ring 18 syndrome. What made her unique was she was also mosaic—which means not all the 18th chromosome was compromised when the she was conceived. There was genetic substance lost which caused the chromosome to spin which caused the ring. When her blood was tested in the genetic lab she had some cells with the ring and some without which made her mosaic. The life expectancy for a child born with ring 18 is five years old, but because Andrea had normal cells she lived until age 31. My husband, Steven, and I believe that the Lord blessed us with 31 years. We miss her every minute of every day but know that we will see her again. That is what keeps us going every day.   -Cathy

Photos provided by Cathy

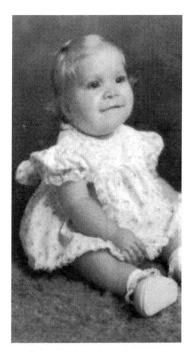

"I bear witness of that day when loved ones whom we knew to have disabilities in mortality will stand before us glorified and grand, breathtakingly perfect in body and mind."[1]

-Jeffrey R. Holland

Note

1. L.D.S. General Conference October 2013 "Like a Broken Vessel"

Whatever it Takes

In the late 90's I became a respite provider for a sweet-looking couple searching for responsible care for their fragile son, Jimmy*. He had cerebral palsy, was very thin, and as intelligent as any four-year-old I'd ever known.

Jimmy quickly learned all our family's names, as well as the names of friends who stopped by now and then. He loved to talk non-stop. He could hear phone conversations in the next room, so we were all on alert to be on our best behavior. No yelling, no swearing (rarely happened, thank goodness), and no gossiping. Jimmy was a sweet, tender-hearted soul. He had no guile. If any-one was injured physically or emotionally, he would often cry for that person.

*Names changed to protect privacy

His mother was attending school earning teaching credentials in special education. She wanted to be positively present during Jimmy's schooling. His father always seemed loving and caring toward his son and wife. Jimmy adored both of his parents, and I sensed he valued their love for him. This attributed to Jimmy's being a very well-adjusted child. He also was fortunate to have his maternal grandparents in his life and living nearby.

One day at lunchtime, Jimmy's mother frantically called to alert me of his accident at preschool, during recess. A special education assistant had forgotten to set Jimmy's wheelchair brakes on, and he had rolled backwards off a curb. I was sad to visualize the severe terror that must have been on Jimmy's sweet, innocent face when he realized what was about to happen, but was helpless to prevent it. His chair fell sideways and Jimmy's face, arm and knee smashed into the asphalt. He wouldn't be coming to my home that day. Thankfully, no bones were broken, but Jimmy was badly scraped up and had three stitches on his forehead.

After that horrific incident, Jimmy became a nervous child. Anyone lifting him would have to do so slowly, assuring him he'd be fine. His parents placed him in a different school which offered a special education class with higher adult-to-pupil ratio.

Jimmy's mother finished her education in a little over one year after the accident and was hired to teach Jimmy's first grade class. Special education teachers are in high demand. I had lost touch of the family at that point because they no longer required respite services. The grandparents helped a lot after school.

Years later my husband, Dan, saw Jimmy's mother at the grocery store. She had divorced her husband after Jimmy's ninth birthday. This mother had gone through great emotional challenges, but Jimmy continued to be a well-adjusted child despite his parents' divorce.

Jimmy is one unique child given every chance to reach his full potential thanks to his strong mother, father, and loving grandparents. I can still hear his sweet squeaky voice, "Hi! Diane Nutz. I'm here!"

A Beauty

We all understand appearances can be misleading. As I mentioned earlier, children who have autism spectrum are usually striking in appearance. Gabrielle was such a child. Her mother had taught her to use sign language at an early age, since Gabrielle   was not able to verbalize her wants and needs. Her signing was   a bit shoddy at age five, but then again, so was mine.

I could transport Gabrielle in my van very easily with her being ambulatory. She enjoyed outings, especially going to activities my children participated in, such as gymnastics, soccer games, and scouting events such as the Pinewood Derby. If she was bored, I would walk around with her or take her to play at a nearby park.

I think all strangers who attempted to make conversation with Gabrielle ended up confused. Perhaps, they wondered what language Gabrielle was fluent in. She obviously didn't comprehend

English. I would have to explain, "She has special needs." Even offering Gabrielle a piece of wrapped candy was futile. She seemed to look right through you and keep walking.

Her single mother changed Gabrielle's places of education as often as became necessary. It can be tricky to find the best teacher for a child such as Gabrielle. Frustration was an emotion that sweet Gabrielle experienced in her daily life. I watched as her mother struggled, trying to provide her daughter with the best chance to achieve something. Her mother found great excitement with small accomplishments. Whenever Gabrielle would try a new food, keep her clothes on all day, or not bang her head on the floor, her mother found it thrilling. Again, I marveled at the courage of another parent of a child with such huge barriers.

Age 5

Gabrielle with her grandfather shortly before he passed away

From Gabrielle's mother:

As a mother of a child with autism, every hug, every "mama," every laugh warms my heart, since she was diagnosed with autism. They had told me she would never do these things. She hugs and kisses her sister and her Adult Disability Home Mom as well. Last time I visited, she loved the dogs too. They came to her and wanted to be touched. She did pet them, and then tried to kiss them. It was so sweet.

-Danielle

Sense or Scents?

Many pet owners realize dogs have a keen sense of awareness when it comes to the needs of their human. This truth really hit home to me, in the case of our mixed terrier, Wally. That animal was more like a person than a dog at times. His sneaky character reminded us of a two-year-old striving for independence when the mother or father wasn't near.

One of many examples is when Wally got into a child's backpack and stole a box of raisins. He must have smelled the raisins even though the small box was hidden deep in the backpack. Unnoticed still, he ate the raisins on a nearby couch, and placed a pillow over the empty box to hide the evidence!

Being accustomed to various people coming and going in the Nutz house, Wally was not the least bit shy. We had a foster child for a couple of years who delighted in torturing animals. He would try to grab Wally by the tail. It only took a couple of instances for Wally to realize, "This human is a walking menace!" Wally would take the long way around to avoid this boy.

A few of the individuals with special needs I cared for through the years while Wally was a member of our family, were afraid of, or didn't like, dogs. That was never a problem for Wally. That smart canine didn't jump or lick on those folks who preferred to avoid him. He paid no mind to them, as if they were invisible. But that didn't mean Wally would ignore their belongings, such as a backpack. He could sniff out a three-day-old peanut butter sandwich if he wanted a snack.

Janel, my high functioning friend with Down syndrome, disliked Wally with a passion. She reminded me often, "Wally stinks like a dog!" "Why won't Wally stop that barking?" "He hurts my ears!" I felt bad for Wally, but there would be no pleasing Janel. Whenever she came, we'd try to keep Wally away from her by putting him outside or in his crate. Of course, his barking didn't quiet because Janel found it objectionable.

My pal, Gabrielle, on the other hand, who had autism, loved our Jack Russell Terrier. That little girl was active and aggressive. Sometimes, she hugged tight to Wally and he *let* her. Whenever she pulled his ears and giggled, Wally endured it. He put up with her roughness because he understood Gabrielle was *special*. Wally made Gabrielle happy, and he seemed to sense that. Or was it her scent that made Wally so easy-going?

Son, Speedy, sparing with his pal Wally

You're the Best!

Between ages 15 to 21, students with special needs attend a local high school. The classes are small compared to a typical classroom and will also include teacher assistants. These students will be taught functional skills, making it possible for some to become independent adults in society to a certain degree.

When Janel was 19 years old, I became her respite provider. Her parents were both employed at the time their daughter attended high school. She had one older brother. This girl had Down syndrome, but I soon learned, was gifted in many ways.

Our youngest son, Speedy, was in junior high at the time. He gained a love of music at an early age. Piano lessons began at age six for Speedy. In elementary school, he played percussion in the school band.

When Speedy started junior high, he found like-minded friends, and they started a rock band called *Hazy*. This was only the start of his musical career. Having a bedroom that faced a busy street, with only one neighbor on the opposite side of the house, worked to his and our advantage. We encouraged the band to practice in his bedroom whenever they wanted. Yes, it was loud, but we loved having them develop their love of music and appropriate friendships. Not to mention, Janel loved the music too.

On many occasions, Janel would venture to the back of the house to peer at the band and rock out in her own style. The four boys in the band went along with her, displaying the gentlest attitude. When she asked if they could play David Bowie, Janel took hold of the microphone and belted out, "HEY MAN…HEY MAN…!" I didn't recognize what they were playing, but rock star Janel was right on cue and loved every minute of it. Other times she would ask to sit behind the drum set and keep a beat to their tunes. It was cute, touching, and amusing. We gave her parents a video recording of these moments. We have watched it over and over again in the course of many years at Janel's insistence. She loves reliving these incredible memories of her few minutes of fame.

Have you ever heard an old song and tried to remember who sang it? This happens to me often, especially if the song was what you call a one-hit wonder. To this day, when Janel is with me, she will recognize the artist 99 percent of the time. Once, as we listened to "Proud Mary" by Credence Clearwater Revival, Janel blurted out, "Hey, Tina Turner sings this too! And she has hot legs!" I inquired how she knew that. She informed me that Rod Stewart says so. Wow. The song, "Hot Legs" by Rod Stewart, came out in 1977. Janel was born in 1979 and is now 38 years old.

Another time as we listened to "Natural Woman" on the radio in my car, Janel informed me, "The Queen of Soul sings this. That's Aretha Franklin!" She hasn't had a memory problem regarding the musical scene, as some of us do.

One occasion last May when Janel came to my house, she announced, "Today is Laura's birthday!" She had total recall of a conversation she'd had with my friend, Laura, a few months earlier. I looked it up and she was spot on. We called Laura so Janel could wish her a happy birthday. Laura was very amazed, as was I, how Janel remembered the exact date of her birthday.

Janel's mother, Janice, told me she was insisting, "Mom, I want to let my hair grow long, like Diane's." Now, for over two years Janel has only been getting only trims every haircut session. Her favorite hairstyle is a side French braid. One year, sporting her side French braid, Janel was dressed up as Elsa, from the movie *Frozen* on Halloween. Every single time Janel's at my home, she insists I secure her hair in one or two French braids 30 minutes before she goes home.

In Janel's world, she is whatever or whomever she chooses. That may be a rock star, cheerleader, or even Elsa from *Frozen.* She knows she is the most beautiful girl in the entire world and the best at whatever she does. Do not feel sorry for her. Her parents have done an amazing job giving their daughter the best life possible. This has involved numerous doctor appointments and some hospital trips to keep on top of health issues.

Hopefully, I haven't given the impression that Miss Janel is a perfect young lady. She has many stubborn moments (her parents know this better than any). Her lupus has complications and affects her moods as well. She has back and kidney problems, sensitivity to hot and cold, loud noises and smells. But then there's that moment when she tells me, after I've braided her hair for the umpteenth time, "Diane, you're the best!"

Janel's braids with Diane and granddaughter Delaney

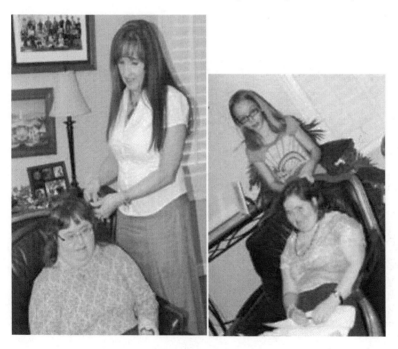

Janel, at a younger age, trying out Grandpa Bailey's motorcycle

Granddaughter Grace and Janel rockin out to dancing Santa

Janel's and Aurelia's pretty toes

From Janel's mother:

When asked if I would write something about my daughter with special needs (a challenging and/or memorable moment), "Sure," was my first response. As I have sat and tried several times to write, there are so many things I want to say, but how do you narrow it down to just a few words?

Thinking back, my first thought was how devastated I felt when I was told my daughter, Janel, had Down syndrome. And now, 38 years later I would say that with so many challenges along the way (medically, physically, socially, and so forth), I have truly been blessed with the most precious gift that God has trusted me with.

Recently, as I was about in tears because of all I had on my plate, I asked Janel to leave me alone for a few minutes. She stopped demanding, abruptly turned around and said, "Fine! Then just shake your bootie!" Needless to say, no more tears for me!

Janel has proven those doctors wrong who, 38 years ago, said that she might never walk, talk, or contribute to society. She is very active socially. She walks, talks (non-stop), writes, types, sings, dances, knows all the musical artists on the radio, actors' names in movies and on television, and will correct you in a heartbeat if you mess up!

Janel has so much personality. She is what keeps me grounded and smiling every day. Janel gives nothing but unconditional LOVE. My personal rewards to this day are my daily hugs, my "love you's" and the constant reminders that she is still my "Very Special Angel".

-Janice

Reason to Celebrate

Misty*, a 16-year-old with Down syndrome, was being raised by her single mother, Kim*. I have come across this a few times, where the other parent was totally missing from the child's life. Most often the absent parent decided they weren't up to the task of raising a special child.

Raising typical children as a single parent presents many obstacles, as I experienced for awhile with four children. But children with disabilities have numerous challenges and the single parent may feel overwhelmed. States provide services mostly based on diagnoses and need. Single parents are usually eligible to receive services such as respite, habilitation, attendant care, speech, and physical therapy for their child with disabilities. Trying to hold down a job and keep up with your child's needs can be

*Names changed to protect privacy

76

quite complicated. Parents I've worked with who are in this situation are determined to love their child unconditionally and provide them with help which gives their child success and happiness. However small that may be, it's worth all the work and effort.

Misty was indeed a bubbly young lady, very outgoing and high functioning. She loved to participate in Special Olympics cheer. The high school cheer team invited the young adults with special needs from the high school to join the cheer squad one evening at a football game. They practiced after school four days ahead of time. The cheer squad helped the challenged girls memorize chants and easy moves. I was touched by the squad's patience and caring attitudes. My daughter, Nikki, being cheer captain, took Misty under her wing and lovingly guided her when needed. Misty was especially excited and she cheered at the top of her lungs.

Not a shy bone in this girl's body, Misty shined personality wise. She was her mother's pride and joy. Besides cheering, Misty could sit for hours viewing horror movies. She found them humorous. Some of the movies she owned could not be shown at my house, because other children (and even some adults) would find them disturbing and end up having nightmares. Not Misty though. She found all that blood and guts hilarious.

One disconcerting incident that shook Misty's mother, Kim, to the core happened when Misty, age 17, was enrolled at the local high school. A special needs bus transported her daily to and from school. There were some mornings when Misty's mother left for work and the bus was later than usual. But Misty would sit by her front door and wait until the bus arrived. This one morning, Kim, had forgotten to take her lunch to work. When she drove home to pick it up around 11 a.m., there was Misty, still sitting, waiting for the bus!

How would you feel if your typical child had sat four hours waiting for the bus? Misty hadn't moved. She knew her bus would arrive, as it always did. It's easy to understand how upset her mother was. Not only did Kim call the bus transportation supervisor, she reported this to the local news channel. They were out the next day interviewing Misty's mother, and they did a short clip with me, as well. Since the bus would leave Misty at my home after school, the news clip showed Misty getting off the bus, smiling merrily.

It seems very likely to me that somebody got fired from their bus driving job after forgetting to pick up the one student. Many worse situations could have occurred. I believe these children must have guardian angels looking after them at times such as this.

Taking Misty out for her first adult drink at age 21 was a grand occasion. Kim had explained to her daughter that the fruity tropical rum drink called "The Bahama Mama" was very tasty. When the waitress asked Misty what she'd like to drink, she told her proudly, "I'll have The Bahama Your Mama."

Kim considered herself blessed to have a daughter with special needs all to herself. A couple of years before Misty's birth, Kim had given birth to a stillborn baby with many birth defects. When Misty was born, Kim was relieved her baby lived to go home with her. This baby brought Kim more bliss than she'd ever envisioned. For Kim, every day since Misty's birth has been a cause for celebration.

A Father's Love

Sometimes you run across an unfamiliar family scenario. Keith* was alone raising his severely mentally and physically handicapped son, Paul*. This time it was the mother who left the family. Thankfully, Keith was gifted with the nurturing instinct to absolutely care for and love his son.

One of the things that stood out to me was the stylish and clean way that Keith dressed and cared for Paul. This eight-year-old boy may not have been aware of his appearance, but everyone else could see what an amazing father Paul had. He wore modern and age-appropriate clothes that were always spotless and appeared quite new. He sported an up-to-date hair style. This little boy had a nice, thick head of hair, always combed and kept.

*Names changed to protect privacy

Paul's prognosis was quite grim at birth. That did not deter Keith from trying his best to raise him. I'm sure most doctors considered it quite miraculous when Paul walked. He wore braces on his legs and needed some help, but he did walk. Keith felt immense pride in his son's accomplishments. Great were this father's rewards.

It is not an easy task to toilet-train most children with special needs, and sometimes, it is impossible. If you've ever had the experience of toilet-training a typical child, you'll agree, that success seems unattainable at times. This father was able, through years of patience, to teach Paul, to use a toilet when assisted. Caregivers, such as me, school teachers and assistants, were given instructions: Set Paul on the toilet every three hours. Stay there and wait about five minutes. Normally Paul would have success, but after five minutes, no matter the results, you'd help him stand, and then assist pulling his pants up.

Paul would seem upset sometimes by practically crying. He could be thirsty, hungry, or need to use the bathroom. I became accustomed to signals from the young boy. Communication comes in various forms. This young man had a father who taught his son in a way his son could learn. And it was extremely noticeable that Paul loved his father because when he arrived to take his son home, Paul responded with outstretched arms and a beaming smile.

Flying Solo

Although every divorced parent I've worked for has raised their child with special needs without the other biological parent's help in any way, I know this is not always the case. I can't help but think, however, that caring for your child with unusual physical and mental characteristics would put an extra strain on a marriage. For those of us raising typical children, we know, even that puts a strain on a marriage at times. It has some challenges!

I checked studies about divorce rates among those raising children with special needs. Recently, I heard that statistics showed a divorce rate of 80 percent,[1] but I could not find documentation to prove it. I had hoped to find a percentage for how many single parents were raising their children with disabilities without any support whatsoever from the other parent, but again, no findings.

The data I found was for three different groups of classified disabilities. Parents who have a child diagnosed with autism spectrum are 23.5 percent more likely to get divorced, compared to typical children at 13.8 percent by the time the child is eight years of age.[2] If a child is diagnosed with ADHD, parents are 22.7 percent more likely to get divorced by the time the child is eight years of age.[3] However, the last group surprised me. Parents of children with Down syndrome are less likely to divorce than families of children with other congenital birth defects by 11.25 percent.[4]

One wonderful attribute of every single parent of a child with special needs that I've cared for, is that none of those parents ever complained about the job they had to do, alone. The singular love of one parent was sufficient for their child. I give them immense credit for their attitude and courage. Since I had been a single parent of four healthy children, I have a deeper respect for such remarkable parents, who seem to survive quite well *Flying Solo*.

NOTES

1. Dr. G., "Special Needs and Divorce: What Does the Data Say?," *Church4EveryChild* (blog), April 12, 2011, https//church4everychild.org/2011/04/12/special-needs-and-divorce-what-does-the-data-say/

2. "Editorial," *Autism* 17, no. 6 (2013): 643-644, doi:10.1177/1362361313509528

3. Brian T. Wymbs, William E. Pelham Jr., Brooke S. G. Molina, Elizabeth M. Gnagy, Tracey K. Wilson, and Joel B. Greenhouse, "Rate and Predictors of divorce among parents of youth with ADHD," *Journal of Consultative Clinical Psychology* 76, no. 5 (October 2008): 735-744, doi:10.1037/a0012719

4. Richard C. Urbano, Robert M. Hodapp and Frank Floyd, "Divorce in Families of Children With Down Syndrome: A Population-Based Study," *American Journal on Mental Retardation*, Vol. 112, No. 4 (July 2007): 261-274

Going Nuts in the Nutz House

As busy as I was, it shouldn't have surprised me that I had a reoccurring dream, or nightmare. I call it my prehistoric dream:

The Pontiac Montana is filled to capacity, or perhaps beyond that. The eight seat belts are securely fastened across occupants' laps. But there are more! My four youngest children, along with several passengers with special needs, crowd my van. Heads hang out windows. Arms fling in every which direction. How in the world did I fit four wheelchairs in here? Oh, and it's loud!

I slowly head out wondering, "What is my destination?" Approaching the vertical hill, I begin to creep up. I suddenly realize there is no engine. My feet slap the pavement beneath my driver's seat. I am in a prehistoric car! I'm wearing my most recent purchase of athletic sneakers hoping their tread will take the beating on the pavement. I must make it to the tip top of this summit, seeing no other choice.

I realize the children (not sure of their numbers) are happily singing, talking or just smiling, since some aren't able to vocalize. My children are helpful and considerate of the children with disabilities that I care for. I am responsible for them all and desire to keep them content and out of harm's way. This is a great mission I face. And I am on my own; it seems, in my task. This road is deserted.

Finally, we reach the top, or tip, and I am about out of breath, but relieved, until, I look down the sharp drop to the bottom of the hill. I had figured that my destination would be, Bedrock, since I was in a prehistoric vehicle. Wrong! At the bottom of the abrupt incline is a placid lake. Yikes, no brakes on this stone age car! The van creaks as it balances on the very top of the tip, but only for a moment. I continue the only direction possible, down, down, down we go.

My head is spinning as I mull over my thoughts, "Which children do I save from drowning? My four children swim rather well, except for my two-year-old who has barely learned to grab the side of the pool. No pool rims down there. It'll be very difficult to disconnect all the belts on any given wheelchair. Oh my! We are so doomed. What a nightmare!"

Yep, it *was* a nightmare. My eyes shoot open! Wow, what a dreadful dream. And why on earth?

This dream returns to my slumber many nights. I'm always able to waken myself before we splash into the lake. If I analyze the scenario, I'm able to grasp some meaning. Yes, I am aware I have taken on a load of responsibility. I seem to thrive on challenges (understatement). My husband and I are raising a combined family of eight children which are many mouths to feed. My job is demanding. I care for individuals with special needs, but I find it gratifying. Each has unique qualities and personalities unlike anyone else. Besides, we all are singular from any other person on this earth. I repeat to myself, sometimes numerous times a day, "I can do this!" But please, no lakes at the end of the road.

In-home respite certification may cover 24 hours per day, or only day, and no overnight coverage. Raising a large family can be costly. In the beginning, I was certified to do overnight work in my home to help our income. Most of the children with special needs that I cared for did not sleep well at night. Besides the extra work, the pay was skimpy, to say the least. The State paid you for (one visit) 11 hours total of up to 24 hours of care. Not only did the provider, me in this case, get the low pay, but the parents would have to claim the total hours their child(ren) were in respite care. Most families were only given 60 hours per month of respite.

Zander*, age 15, was a client I had in my home overnight on a few occasions. Zander's parents would leave him in my care 24 hours or more if they went out of town. I would get paid for 11 of every 24 hours. Even though I only got paid for 11 hours, his parents would have used 24 hours of their allowable monthly respite time.

We had a fold-out bed in our family room where Zander would sleep. He wasn't ambulatory (wheelchair bound), was non-verbal, and blind. I changed his diapers and fed him. He loved music, as most of my clients did. We had three children who had become very proficient on the piano. They really loved to practice. This

*Names changed to protect privacy

was due, I think, to the competition taking place between these two daughters and one son. Zander was thus easily entertained when these three were around; fighting over whose turn it was to bust out some tunes on our piano. We were amused as Zander's hands would continually fly back and forth to the beat of the music. He had his own singing style as well, which could be distracting when he turned his volume up.

On this weekend, Zander was our guest from Friday to Sunday evening. An hour after his high school bus dropped him off at my residence, Zander began to giggle! We didn't know to what we owed this pleasure. I moved him to a different room, but his loud laughter continued. He didn't get much rest between his laughing outbursts. It was difficult to feed him while he tried desperately to control his fits of laughter. This was a new challenge for me. How do you help a child stop laughing? I have struggled at times with getting a child with special needs to even smile. This nervous chuckle was wearing on me and my family.

Calling the parents was the option I hoped to not use. They were on an anniversary vacation and of course didn't acquire many weekend retreats. Having explained the problem to his mother, she told me this had never happened to him. She was not concerned in the least. The poor guy was beginning to cry during outbursts of laughing, with frustration. If he wasn't in any pain, his mother was comfortable with his ongoing giggling.

All night, I kept thinking, surely Zander would wear out and get some sleep, but that didn't happen. Being a light sleeper, I was also awake. The rest of my family slumbered peacefully as I lay awake listening to the unending snickers, failing to find any humor in it. When all was said and done, Zander had laughed aloud over 12 hours! Being exhausted, he kept dozing off all day Sunday.

His parents, being refreshed after a wonderful weekend getaway, noticed how tired Zander was upon their arrival. The only explanation his mother could figure was perhaps the school nurse on Friday gave Zander someone else's medication and it caused an unusual seizure. The young teen did suffer from minor seizures during the day, which I charted for his parents. But this was completely out of the norm for him. Poor innocent Zander had literally laughed until he cried.

I no longer offer overnight care. Sometimes it weighs heavy on my heart, because the parents of these unique children require some free time to lift their spirits and tired bodies. Being in my sixties now, however, I need that rest time as well. I wonder if Zander ever thinks about being in the Nutz home and cracks a smile or a loud chuckle.

Alarmed!

I'm sure we weren't the only family to get suckered into receiving a so-called *free* home alarm system. You know how it goes, yep, free set up of equipment to show off to the neighbors. But take my advice; don't forget to read the fine print where it states you only pay so much per month for three years (and no less than that). We signed on the dotted line, they hooked us.

When there are several people living in your home, plus many special visitors, it may not be easy to place blame on who left the front door unlocked. Any person entering and not aware of the alarm code could become victim to the dreaded, high pitched, shrill beeping. Next, an unidentified, live operator comes on the intercom asking for the code word. If you could remember the code word, or even knew what it was to begin with, and could say it to her, the awful sound would stop.

*Names changed to protect privacy

I had almost reached home, when a client with special needs named, Roxy*, arrived via school bus. The usual non-punctual bus had come, early, of course, on the one day I was running five minutes late from my other job.

Roxy's appearance differed from a typical 16-year-old girl. Her left arm was noticeably shorter than her right. She had scoliosis. Her smile was large with rotting teeth. Her voice was loud enough, but her pronunciation was not always clear enough for the listener to comprehend every word. She wore bright yellow cowgirl boots and wouldn't hesitate to kick anyone who teased or upset her. However, this girl was playfully comical and very spunky. Her inner person would be unrecognizable to a casual passerby.

Most school bus drivers follow rules, helping to keep their precious cargo safe. The schedules they keep are quite tight and punctual. This ensures they keep to the scheduled pick up and drop off times. This day was one of the exceptions. The bus arrived early, and the bus driver had not followed one of the most important rules. He left the student at my home before catching even a glimpse of an adult present to supervise.

Upon arrival, Roxy knocked. Probably rather quickly, she opened the door, which someone had left unlocked. The home alarm blared. Since I was not home yet, I can only imagine how bewildered Roxy was when the noise began. First, she got flustered, mad and scared, partly because any loud noises were magnified in her head. Then a lady's earsplitting voice pierced Roxy's acute hearing.

"Ms., please give me your pass code!" Roxy tried to speak, "Himma, gopy, clood, rasst, *&##****!" (Oh, and the swear words Roxy knew were spoken loud and clear.) Then the alarm operator tried again, "Please talk clearly Ms. I can't understand you. I need your pass code." Roxy blubbered once again, "Whatter, imorrror! Unkeryitermin! *+*?//+**###!!!"

When I arrived, I parked in the garage and entered the kitchen door to a scene I never expected to find. Feeling perplexed, I calmed Roxy down and spoke with the disconcerted operator, giving her our password. That annoying alarm finally subsided. I found it difficult not to laugh at what had just happened!

Unofficial Officer

The town of Guadalupe, being a tightly knit community, consisted mainly of Hispanics and Native Americans. Students were bused to the Tempe School District. A few of the students in our classroom understood two languages, Spanish and English.

Perhaps, the most entertaining young man in our class was Jose*. He was adopted at age two by a loving couple and now was eight years old. Jose was mesmerized by tires. Any tire. But seeing large truck or tractor tires especially energized him. Jose verbalized extremely well, in English or Spanish.

Whenever we three adult leaders ventured off campus on a field trip with the nine students, it was anything but boring. One of our very important duties was to point out any monster tires in the vicinity. However, Eagle Eye Jose usually noticed them before we did.

*Names changed to protect privacy

Not only did Jose have an unquenchable thirst to find tires, but this hobby included road cones and portable signs of road work. His mother told us an amusing story about a knock that came to her door one Saturday afternoon. A policeman was alerting her to the fact that Jose was at it again. His collection of road cones was set up in front of his house redirecting traffic in a most peculiar way. Several vehicles were lined up on a dead-end road. The police in Guadalupe knew Jose alright, the *Unofficial Officer.* They were fortunate to witness the puzzled motorists that Saturday afternoon.

Appear Typical

Kjera sent this to me about her ongoing education with her children:

Both of my children have been diagnosed with multiple disabilities. Since they appear perfectly typical in appearance, it creates difficulties from outsiders who lack understanding and knowledge of the very real challenges we face daily.

Connor is 14 years of age. At age three he was diagnosed with OCD. When he was five years old he was also diagnosed with autism, ADHD and anxiety. Under his diagnoses of autism he has executive functioning and sensory issues.

My daughter, Rylee, will soon be 12 years old. When she was barely two months old, she was diagnosed with failure to thrive. At age five she was diagnosed with Asperger's syndrome and ADHD. Under her Asperger's syndrome she also has executive functioning issues. At age ten it was discovered that a lot of her

ADHD symptoms were caused by major deficits in every sensory category. That same year she was diagnosed with dyslexia. The executive functioning issues qualify as a cognitive disability.

The struggle is real. Let me explain a little bit of my children's world, just a tiny part of their multiple disabilities. Let's take a walk through what goes on in part of the way their brain works:

Executive functions consist of several mental skills that help the brain organize and act on information. These skills enable people to plan, organize, remember things, prioritize, pay attention and get started on tasks. They also help people use information and experiences from the past to solve current problems.

If your child, like mine, has executive functioning issues, any task requiring these skills could be a challenge. That could include doing a load of laundry or completing a school project. Having issues with executive functioning makes it difficult to:

Keep track of time
Make plans
Make sure work is finished on time
Multitask
Apply previously learned information to solve problems
Analyze ideas
Look for help or more information when it is needed

What can happen is they may start a task such as laundry but forget steps such as put the soap in with the water. Or they can do things out of order like put the clothes in the washer but forget to turn on the water. As my children get older, after a lot of repetition working with them, they can now catch themselves skipping steps. They still skip steps but they are more aware of themselves. If you see me looking frazzled, with a lack of energy, or if I say it's a lot of work helping my children, you'll understand this outcome bet-ter. I have to supervise every task they do all day long. It is listed under cognitive control. We are still working on the concept of time and learning from the past. But we can do it!

This website helps me put things simply for others to understand:

https://www.understood.org/en/learning-attention-issues/child-learning-disabilities/executive-functioning-issues/understanding-executive-functioning-issues

-Kjera

Photos provided by Kjera

Connor's Eagle Scout board of review

Rylee's Special Olympics Cheer and Track

97

The Tasty Onion

Over the many years, a few clients remain in my memory because of their unique personalities. I share a few amusing experiences mainly because these stories seem to enlighten and bring joy to my audience.

A young boy of age nine, Stewart* came to my home for after-school care for approximately three years. Being short for his age and wearing thick glasses, his appearance reminded me of Sherman on the old cartoon *Mr. Peabody and Sherman*. Stewart's mother or father would pick him up within two hours, on their way home from work. His parents preferred that I not transport Stewart since he suffered from grand mal seizures at least twice a year. There was always medication in his backpack in case this happened in my home. I would administer to Stewart the life-saving prescription rectally. This allows quicker release into his system.

*Names changed to protect privacy

We were all fortunate that Stewart never suffered a seizure while in my care. I had heard the school nurse followed treatment instructions successfully and an ambulance was always called for follow-up care.

Having medical problems since birth, Stewart was developmentally delayed. He struggled with writing because he lacked hand-eye coordination, and math logic problems. Having a fear of physical play, he would sometimes be left out of games on the playground with his peers. I assumed his parents instilled in him often the need to *be careful*. Stewart's appreciation for kindness from others his age was greater than most of us. He shared some of his experiences with me, such as a boy inviting him to play basketball with him. This almost brought tears to Stewart's eyes as he relived the happy incident with me.

Reading the dictionary was this young boy's favorite past-time. This seemed to be his main enjoyment in my home. As soon as he walked through the front door, he would announce, "Hi Diane! I'm here! Can I read your dictionary?" There he'd sit for at least 30 minutes, at my kitchen table, reading the large book. I noticed he always opened it to a different section. Stewart taught *me* a few vocabulary words. He delighted in educating me.

One early evening as I was preparing to chop up a large white onion for a stir-fry dish, Stewart plopped the dictionary on the kitchen table and walked up to me. Starring at the onion at about eye-level, he asked, "What is that?" When I told him what it was, he said he never heard of an onion. Even though I warned him that most children do not like to eat onions, he insisted on trying it and grabbed it out of my hand! Luckily, I had already washed the skin off. My eyes widened as I stared at Stewart taking a large bite out of this whole onion. I was ready to pour him a quick glass of milk or water, until he said, "Hmmmm, not bad." Two more bites followed and then he declared, "Okay, that's enough. Thanks! That was, ummm, that was, delectable! That's a word I learned today in your dictionary!"

Warning Stewart's mother when she arrived, that her son most likely had very bad breath, I filled her in on the surprising news that he loves whole, raw onions. She was very perplexed by that update. And now remember, an onion is *delectable!*

The Musical Eagle

Reading my son's Eagle Scout project, which follows, brought back to my mind the many hours Speedy spent preparing the music clinic. It was a rewarding endeavor for him. I was able to get in touch with a few of the participants, even though it's been over 11 years. Here are some of their comments:

Chelsey told me she still has the cd and especially enjoys the Beatles song on it. She wishes she could remember making the Guitar Box! The class about music and structure actually taught her more than she already knew, and she had fun singing in the voice class.

Aurelia's mother said it brings a smile to her face as she remembers the thrill her daughter got when she won the cute balloon door prize. And her son, Lloyd, just smiled through the whole clinic. She felt it benefited her children with special needs to be included in such a fun activity.

Another participant was Janel, who proudly displays her music clinic certificate of completion on her bedroom wall to this very day. She remembers how yummy the cookies were and still has the cd.

Rick, one of the adult helpers told me that it was always fun to get in on Speedy's music career as it advanced. He especially liked the idea Speedy had to help younger children learn about music, including those with disabilities. Because many years have gone by, Rick can't recall the details, but he does remember a good feeling, and that's what counts. He said that Speedy did a good thing helping people, and put smiles on their faces with his Eagle Scout project.

Written by K. Speedy Nutz:

Looking back at the Eagle Scout project I completed at 17 years old, I realize now (at the old age of 28) how much my mom influenced my choice to work on something very different from the usual Eagle Scout project. Typically, scouts set such goals as collecting 200 books for a library or painting park benches. I wanted to do something that would benefit people who are sometimes missed or not thought about. A project that would help children with disabilities would be easier for me since my parents could help because of their background, especially my mom's.

The foremost responsibility of an Eagle Shout in the Boy Scouts of America is to live with honor, loyalty, courage, cheerfulness and to serve. The Eagle stands as a protector of the weak and helpless. I felt the project I had in mind would accomplish all of the above objectives.

I thought of my talents and what I could do with them to make a successful Eagle Scout project. I'm a fairly decent musician, so my project would include music which would help all children but focus mainly on those with special needs.

The perfect project seemed to be a musical clinic for children, and to encourage those with mental and physical challenges to participate. I had already learned many things about music therapy and the wonders it does for people, and felt this project would be very beneficial for that particular group.

My proposal stated that my objective was to hold a music clinic for children. My main purpose was to include those children with special needs. I had grown up with various types of unique guests spending time in our home. Since I was accustomed to interacting with people who had special needs, it was not a big deal to me. Because of my mom's job, I was comfortable with people whom others were sometimes afraid of or uncomfortable with.

I first talked with my scout leader about what I would need to do. In the end we decided that we would pass out fliers which would explain what my music clinic was all about to special needs classes. I would arrange five different stations, or classes, in my clinic. The classes would be called: Instrument Making, Theory and Structure, Singing, Movements/Types of Music, and Types of Instruments. The flier would illustrate how I wanted to focus on making the clinic educational and fun at the same time.

The perfect place for my project would be my church building, since there were classrooms and larger rooms. I would have to call and get clearance for their use. There would be a beginning introduction and an ending performance and closing. My plan was to have at least five instructors, including myself, two volunteers for each class, and others willing to help with organizing and planning the event. Refreshments would be offered at the end of the music clinic.

Lastly, I needed to know where I could find people to attend my clinic. I wrote down the names of schools, classes, and programs where I could pass fliers out.

Once my basic outline was written out, I needed to get approval from a higher scout leader. I remember how excited I was when I turned it in. Since this was a very different type of Eagle Scout project, I remember being nervous as well. As the leader read my proposal, he grinned and said, "Hmmm, an Eagle Scout project in the arts. Go for it!" He told me as far as he knew this type of Eagle project had never been done. Being relieved that I received approval for my project, my level of excitement increased.

My project required a lot of materials. My list included 12 whistles, flutes, harmonicas, clappers, kazoos, balloons, plastic noise makers, and ratchets. I also purchased cookies, cups for water, Mylar balloons, and rubber bands. The Pepsi plant, where my dad was employed at the time, donated 35 boxes. Instruments I used in my clinic included: piano, keyboard, didgeridoo, recorders, trumpet, accordion, drum set, and marimbas. Most of these came from my home. I bought construction paper, tape, stickers, markers, and crayons. In the end, I spent thirty-one dollars I had earned by teaching piano lessons and taking care of someone's pool.

At first I attempted to pass fliers out at a nearby work center for people with disabilities, but after a misunderstanding regarding scheduling, it turned out they were no help to me. This was a major stumbling block, but I decided to email several parents, and I contacted others in person. After realizing I had too many spaces left open, I had volunteers help me pass my fliers out in the neighborhood. I invited local children to my music clinic, which would be well supervised by several adults. (This was before social media was available.)

For my instructors to become experienced, I put together two training sessions for the five teachers. Four of them were given a written lesson planned out by me. The singing leader would prepare her lesson because I had no experience in voice. At each training session I helped each volunteer get an idea of the level at which they should teach.

The Instrument Making class was going to put together what I called a Box Guitar. Each child would get a rectangular shaped box with a pre-cut hole in it. They would be assisted in placing rubber bands over the holes and using short wood dowels as bridges to replicate a guitar. Then they could color and decorate the Box Guitar as they wished.

Theory and Structure was the class I would teach to help the children understand a bit about reading music and the structure of it. They would learn the basics, such as where to find middle C, the names of musical terms, and some rhythmic patterns.

I predicted that the Singing Class would be the most enjoyable for the participants. Each student would have fun singing simple scales, the ABC song, and other easy tunes if able. If some children weren't capable of singing, they would still enjoy listening.

In Movements/Types of Music class, the instructor taught about African and tribal music, Renaissance music, classical music, modern jazz, Rock 'n Roll, and contemporary themes. I burned a compact disc for each child to take home with these songs as a demonstration of each style of music: African Beat, Renaissance music, Ode to Joy, a song by the Beatles, a popular song from The Lion King movie, Sweet Child of Mine, Improvisation Jazz, a song by Lone Star, a song from Star Wars, and the Super Mario theme song.

My dad, who taught the Types of Instrument class, using the instruments provided, demonstrated how each instrument works and sounds. On the display in that class were the brass, woodwind, percussion, and string instruments.

Upon completion of my Eagle Scout project plans and training of the volunteers, the music clinic was ready to commence! It was held at my church in separate rooms I called classes or stations. At the very beginning, we all met in a large room where each child received a name tag with a group name on it. We dismissed each group to follow their group leader to the first class/station. The classes rotated after no certain amount of time. I had a volunteer judge when to ring the bell, depending on how far each class had progressed.

Almost two and a half hours later, we all met back in the same large room in which we had started. I played a jazz piano piece for everyone. My dad played Chopsticks on two recorders at the same time and my mom demonstrated a short song on the accordion. One of my friends played trumpet for awhile. I finished off the show with some beats on a drum set.

For the closing of the music clinic I held a raffle where a child won a fancy balloon. The winner happened to be one of my mom's clients with special needs and she was very excited! Each child was given a gift bag with a variety of plastic instruments, noise makers and so forth. I handed to each child as they were leaving, a balloon, a cookie, a certificate of excellence for attending the clinic, and also their very own original homemade Box Guitar, and made sure they had their compact disc.

Besides the reward I received of becoming an Eagle Scout, I felt well compensated for my time and effort seeing the participant's enjoyment. I had expected twelve to show up; only two having disabilities. Ended up, I had double that in attendance. There were 24 children at my music clinic with eight of them having a mental/physical disability. The music clinic was a tremendous success!

Not only did all of the participants enjoy themselves, but they learned many new things about music. After the clinic, it gave me great satisfaction to tell each smiling child good-bye. All of the volunteers benefited from my music clinic as well. They learned tolerance for children with disabilities. We all gained knowledge while having fun. I also noticed how proud my parents were.

Looking back at the pictures and video clips I have from that eventful day reminds me of the good I did for each of those who participated in their own special way as they assisted me in earning my Eagle Scout award.

-Speedy

Speedy instructing

A volunteer teaching a class

A special student, Lloyd

Collage of Eagle project

Eagle award with parents

Speedy with sisters, Nikki and Dana

Chelsey-isms

Back in the year 2000, when she was 12 years old, Chelsey was thrust into the unknown and uncertainty of a new life. The youngest child of four and suffering from mental delays, no sense of smell, and being legally blind because she was born 13 weeks prematurely, Chelsey relied heavily on her mother's companionship and help. Suddenly her mother suffered a heart attack and was gone from sight.

It's difficult for most to comprehend how the loss of a mother affects a child with special needs. She was Chelsey's advocate for education and physical needs. Everyone in the family relied on their mother/wife to care for the youngest and had taken for granted the intense work and patience required in meeting Chelsey's ongoing needs.

As I interviewed Chelsey for this book, and listened to and observed this sharp, 29-year-old woman, it seemed to me like she was stuck in a time warp. Chelsey has a strong desire to never grow old. Watching the same television shows such as the *Rugrats* cartoons is one example. But you'll never catch Chelsey in front of the television when *Boy Meets World* is on as she despises it.

We went on to discuss her favorite topic of party planning. Her mother was the master of all party planners. Chelsey hopes to become as talented with this job as her mother was.

As a young child, Chelsey loved to sing in front of an audience. During our interview, she said she wanted to write her own songs. She complained that nobody wants to hear her sing or let her perform in a talent show. Her frustration is apparent to me, but her father and siblings are caring for and keeping Chelsey safe to the best of their abilities.

I find Chelsey to be quite typical in other aspects of her life. She loves all chocolate, a gal after my own heart! Other favorite foods are: pizza, spaghetti, barbecue foods, and any type of sausage. She really hates dogs, but likes cats. Going horseback riding is something she misses since her family hasn't done that in quite a while.

One of my questions put an incredibly wide grin on this young lady's face. I asked her, "How has your birth changed the world?" It took her a few minutes and her oldest sister reminded her how entertaining she is. Then Chelsey related to me that it's because of her that her family is not as boring.

I was informed by Chelsey that her mother introduced her to the Beatle's music at a very young age. "Let it Be" is her favorite song. Her brother doesn't play guitar much anymore, but she especially liked when he jammed to tunes by the Beatles. She said, "He's just too busy now and doesn't have time. Life is just mean like that sometimes."

Even though Chelsey loves attention, she is basically quite shy. One of her fears is to be alone. Perhaps her mother's death magnified this apprehension. She thinks about her mother almost every day. As she got a little teary eyed, I asked her if she was okay and she replied, "Yeah, it's not that bad anymore. I'm only crying on the inside." Chelsey thinks everyone deserves a chance to prove themselves. People should not cut others out of activities. She said, "I hope to conquer my fears one day."

I had a brief conversation with her father about some amusing things Chelsey has said. When Chelsey was around age 11, her parents took her on short hike in the mountains. They were walking along a dirt trail when they came to a fork in the road. As her parents were discussing which way to continue, Chelsey had a stick and was digging in the road. When her father asked her what she was doing, she exclaimed, "I am trying to find that fork in the road!"

Her father used to encourage her to stand up straight to improve her posture. Chelsey eventually retorted, "I'm trying to think about that and it just hurts my brain too much. So, I'm not going to think about it anymore."

A visit from Chelsey's 80-year-old aunt and uncle was another memorable occasion. Her relatives met her in the entrance hall and greeted her with, "Hello Chelsey!" And she returned the welcome with, "Hi, you are elderly. Ummm, never mind. My dad doesn't want me to use that word. You are mature. My dad is not mature."

One Sunday, Chelsey was sitting in the hallway outside her Sunday school class. She spotted the bishop strolling toward her. Mumbling under her breath, Chelsey stated in a very matter of fact way, "Oh great. Here comes the king of boring."

Chelsey had a major concern. She related to me, "I've made a huge mistake and I need to fix it as soon as possible. I borrowed money from my dad to help me pay for my Nintendo Switch. Since I don't have a job, how will I ever pay him back? I'll never buy anything online again! I feel so guilty. I can't believe I got myself into this situation." We discussed ways in which she could make money to pay her father back, such as having a bake sale. This put a huge smile on her face.

Within three weeks after the interview, we had two successful bake sales and she was able to pay her father back. All of us need to feel we have purpose in our lives. This experience gave Chelsey a sense of purpose and fulfillment. The people in my neighborhood were very generous by giving her substantial tips on every purchase. Our baking projects included *No Bake Cookies, Powdered Sugar Cookies, and Chewy Chocolate Brownies.*

Very recently Chelsey went with a family friend to volunteer packing rice for hungry children. Being rather annoyed with having to wear a hairnet and struggling to push all the loose hairs inside of it, she requested the friend to assist her. Then she asked, "Do they think I have eyes in the back of my head or something?"

Finding social groups and activities where Chelsey may flourish and move on in her life is a goal her father and siblings share. She continues to be a bright spot and at the same time a challenge to them. I think Chelsey will always be young at heart.

Chelsey

Successful bake sales

No Costume Needed

After my interview with Chelsey, her family asked for my services. There is much to work on with her and it is a slow process. However, witnessing any improvement is rewarding. I respect the privacy of my clients and won't share personal matters. There are some wonderful moments, as well as amusing things that I would like to share. It's my goal to enlighten people who've not had opportunity to converse with *special* people.

I am still learning after all these years myself. The two dances I've taken Chelsey to have been most enjoyable and educational for me, but I believe, more-so for her. That was the main purpose of attending.

The first dance was a Hello dance, where participants were instructed to wear crazy outfits. Her father and I both encouraged her to play along. Chelsey chose to wear two different shoes, a shirt on backwards that read "Everyone makes mistakes", and pants that clashed with her shirt. She stayed on the dance floor almost the whole two hours! She knew a lot of dances such as The Cha Cha Slide, The Macarena, and The Chicken Dance. When I asked her later how she knew all those moves, she replied, "It's from all those school and church dances I used to go to, and about a dozen wedding receptions in my life."

This was my first experience attending a dance for developmentally delayed individuals. Wow, was I missing out all these years! It would be great to be as non-judgmental and fun-loving. There were ages 18 to around 40 I'd guess. Most are childlike, making it difficult to figure out how old they really are.

The Halloween dance was in a much larger building than the Hello dance and had approximately three times as many participants. It also lasted 30 minutes longer and a photo booth was added to the package. Everyone I saw was enjoying the evening and friendly to anyone they came in contact with. Most of them danced alone, but not really. Usually these unique individuals moved around from one group or person to another and interacted. The only time there were wallflowers was when someone was tired out or wanted some punch or treats. There were some in wheelchairs on the dance floor as well, having a blast.

It seemed that Chelsey was the only one not wearing a costume. She was extremely angry when I picked her up to go to the dance. This isn't unusual for her. She tends to magnify that attitude when she gets in the mood. I think her family is more patient than anyone else would be. People have asked me how I can be so patient with some of my clients. My answer is always the same, "It's only a few hours. They don't live with me."

Since Janel's mom, Janice, is more familiar with these activities, I tagged along learning from her experiences. Arriving at the dance, we searched until we found an available table near the right front of the room to park our water bottles and such. Immediately after that, Chelsey and Janel went straight to the dance floor. Janel had a few friends there and when I went out to the dance floor, she introduced them to me. The boy in the horse costume with the large plush head was the first.

There were some creative and elaborate costumes, such as the Horse. Others wore a more simplified costume such as a superhero t-shirt. As I speak of individuals in attendance, I will call them by their character names of the costumes they wore. Janel was a bat, Cutest Bat Ever. Chelsey was just plain Chelsey, Girl in the Green Shirt. Was she embarrassed? Not at all. Did anyone judge her harshly because of her lack of Halloween spirit? Again, no. They did not care, and they had more fun because of it. Chelsey was in her element again, dancing away to the beat of the music. Familiar songs would create a wide smile on her face for a moment. Now, that's gratifying.

As I stood in the photo booth line to save places for the Girl in the Green Shirt and Cutest Bat Ever, I was intrigued with conversations around me. Spiderman and Supergirl were behind me telling each other how everyone noticed they *really* were superheroes. I could clearly hear them, even over the loud music, as they were very excited. They related to each other how some people asked if they were the real deal, and that it was so cool that the authentic Supergirl and Spiderman came to this dance! Every now and then, Spiderman would give me a nudge to move up if it only meant two inches. (Luckily, no super strength was used on me!)

The group of three boys and one girl in front of me in the photo booth line acted like they were fresh out of high school, which would be at least age 21. The Maid, a young lady, seemed very popular with Cyclops Eye, Hercules, and the Mummy. This scantily dressed Maid was quite pretty. Her goal was to go to the nearby community college. But Cyclops Eye had her beat. He was *attending* BYU Idaho, taking psychiatry. He excitingly told his friends, "The Psych department there is the best!" Hercules couldn't believe that Cyclops Eye was able to get into BYU Idaho. Mummy didn't have much to say, possibly because a lot of white rags wrapped around his face made it difficult to speak. Once again I was reminded; the dream world these unique individuals live in is *reality* to them.

After the photo booth pictures, Girl in the Green Shirt told me she was going back out to dance. No surprise to me. I watched her head out to boogie. When she was almost in her place, I proceeded to go sit at *our* table where I could supervise her.

When I glanced around the dance floor, I could not spot Girl in the Green Shirt. I knew she was out there. Where else would she be? Janice and I strolled around looking for the only girl in a green shirt. I admit feelings of concern entered my heart. I checked out the doors that led to a restroom and no luck. After maybe five minutes of searching (which seemed much longer) for Girl in the Green Shirt, thankfully, Janice found her hunched over in a chair at a different table. Hey, if you decide you want to sit down, why does it really matter which table you sit at? No rules were broken, no harm done, only if you count my sometimes over-anxious self!

I'm becoming more aware of the ease with which most people with special needs live their life. There is less pride, and less concern over what anyone else thinks. There are lessons to be learned here.

Spending more time dancing with my two pals, gave me an easier route to supervise my friend, Girl in the Green Shirt, as well as have fun with Cutest Bat Ever.

A pretty little Wonder Woman joined us for several songs and had a difficult time mimicking Girl in the Green Shirt's dance moves. Wonder Woman told us she was 12 years old. I thought her numbers were just mixed up. More like 21.

Cave Woman introduced herself to us as she swung her large plastic dinosaur bone around and almost bopped me in the head. She didn't stay long, as she had more hunting to do.

I tried conversing with Cat Woman when she joined our group. She was really into the act though and only meowed. I don't speak "cat" and she got bored and moved on. *Meow*.

I noticed that the tall thin Frankenstein and the small Hulk would dance with several different people, including Girl in the Green Shirt and Cutest Bat Ever, but I never saw either one of them open their mouth to speak. There are no words needed sometimes.

It was getting slightly warm, so I told the two girls I'd retrieve some drinks and treats for them. Janice and I fetched Girl in the Green Shirt and Cutest Bat Ever some lemonade, cookies, and fish crackers. Before Girl in the Green Shirt could finish her pumpkin shaped cookie, very TALL Superman approached her chair and said something to her. She then looked at me and said, "I think he's trying to get my attention." I heard him then politely ask her if she wanted to dance. I nudged her and told her to go on! She looked at Superman and said, "I don't even know you, but okay."

The six foot eight inch Superman gently took Girl in the Green Shirt by the hand and led her out to dance. After a minute, Flapper Girl (style from the 50's) joined them and all three were happily holding hands, dancing. Girl in the Green Shirt was the first one, it looked like, to let go of hands and dance on her own. The other two followed her lead, dancing separate now with no hard feelings. Janice and I laughed at the delightful scene.

While Cutest Bat Ever and Girl in the Green Shirt were hopping and moving to *Thriller* with me, Sally (*Nightmare Before Christmas*) began a conversation, "Hi! I'm Sally! And me and Jack won the costume contest!" I told her how pretty she was and that I knew (seriously) they would win since they're the best lookin Jack and Sally I'd ever seen. She said, "I know," and flipped her red yarn hair in my face as she quickly turned around to dance, or brag, elsewhere. Cutest Bat Ever gave me a little poke and said, "Hey, come on Diane! Thriller's still on. Dance!"

The last amusing conversation I remember before we left the Halloween dance happened while I was still dancing with my two pals, Girl in the Green Shirt and Cutest Bat ever. Granny came and notified me she needed to leave soon. I asked her why, as there were 30 minutes left. She confided happily, "It's almost time to take the medicine my mom gives me. It's called Miralax and I need to drink it every night." I said, "Oh okay. Tastes pretty gross, huh?" Granny replied, "It's not that bad when you mix it with Gatorade. I kinda like it!" And she was gone and I assumed, on her way to have a *moving* experience.

The dance had come to an end and we gathered our water bottles, as Girl in the Green Shirt gathered the bite-sized assorted chocolate candies on the tables. I'm not sure how many she fit in her pockets, but she did clean off at least two of the round large tables. Oh, how I wish I had the guts to do that!

On the way home Chelsey, Girl in the Green Shirt, told me something at least three times that had her in awe. She had seen two little people at the dance and they must have been as tall as she was at age six. She said, "It's gotta be so hard as an adult to be that short! I can't imagine! Now that's sad." Oh my goodness, the *Chelsey-isms* are never ending. Thank you, Girl in the Green Shirt, for making this world not so boring!

Girl in the Green Shirt   Cutest Bat Ever

Diane and pals

4

Aging in Style

*Meeting and working with individuals
struggling through
everyday obstacles has widened my
awareness and opened my heart to be
accepting of their differences.*

Adult Children

The past 30 years have been a learning journey for me while caring for individuals with special needs. They've been newborn to 40-ish years old. Some are overgrown children in adult bodies, which can be challenging. If they are ambulatory, it helps in some ways. However, if the individual is low functioning *and* ambulatory, there can be trials which may be dangerous for that person. They lack understanding of harmful situations.

Some of you living in a stressful moment with your little ones or teenagers may say, "I can't wait until my children grow up!" It is inevitable, most parents will know of that freedom. However, many will miss their babies after they move on, and perhaps will lose their own individual identity in the process.

My husband Dan and I treasured family vacations and cheering on our children at their various competitions and concerts. We marveled at how blessed we were to witness their achievements as well as their rough learning experiences. Since they've all grown up, and moved out, and most are now raising families of their own, we've grown closer to them emotionally. This should be the ordinary life occurrences when you have children.

I've learned to appreciate our family situation immensely since working with people with special needs and getting acquainted with some of their parents. Most of these parents have a life-time of raising a child(ren) with physical and/or mental disabilities. Their responsibility is never ending. It's their normal. It becomes painfully impossible at times to get needed rest when caring for a special offspring. It is such demanding work.

To illustrate how looks can be deceiving, on one occasion upon returning home from work, Dan saw an unfamiliar guy sitting on our couch watching television. Assuming he was visiting one of our older children, Dan walked up to him, held out his hand, and said, "Hi, I'm Dan." The reaction he received was not expected. The unknown guest flapped his arms and excitingly mumbled something unintelligible. As Dan stared, the young man held out his hand to show Dan a toy race car.

Right as I walked in the room to explain, Dan stepped back and gave me the most comical look. He asked, "One of your new clients I assume? Or did you instruct him to play dumb as a joke when I got home?" Surprisingly, Daryl* looked like any other high school senior. But as you can tell, he was not. He was ambulatory, but non-verbal, and he would never be able to live independently.

*Names changed to protect privacy

Another high school student with questionable future potential to live independently was Terry*. He suffered several seizures every day. Terry could administer his own medications. He set his watch's timer to go off for the specific time each medicine was to be taken. He wore a fanny pack holding his medications. I would monitor as he seized, and time each one, taking notes to give his parents.

Holding a conversation about cars was one of Terry's favorite past times. Traveling in my van, he would point out a favorite car and tell me the model and make. I only traveled with Terry occasionally as his seizures were unpredictable. He also recognized movie stars while he watched television. If I couldn't remember a name of a character on a movie we viewed, he would tell me.

Terry spent most of his day, sitting. If he sat on one side of the couch and suffered one of his terrible seizures, he sometimes ended up on the other side of the couch. The force was that strong. Afterward he needed to nap for about half an hour. These seizures took the energy out of him. It was such a shame the doctors could not get Terry's seizures under control. I doubted he would ever be able to live on his own since he requires supervision for his medical needs.

*Names changed to protect privacy

The agencies I worked for sent me to the client's home now and then. Usually the person was an adult with disabilities living independently, but needed some assistance. Trudy* was a feisty 32-year-old woman residing in an apartment near my home. Born with cerebral palsy, Trudy spent most of her days in a wheelchair, but could cook her meals and take a bus for transportation.

I've found over the years that when I work in an individual's home, most are very particular about how I do chores for them. Trudy was no exception. After I swept her modest living quarters, she'd ask if I remembered to get a certain corner of the room. I'd always comply, trying to smile and redo my chore to make my client content. Other times, I'd be off the hook from her nit-picking when Trudy dozed off. She loved watching old movies late at night.

Being mentally high functioning, Trudy decided to search for a job. I was working for her when she received the call for a job opening at Wal-Mart, as a greeter. She was quite overjoyed and looked forward to such a piece-of-cake job. I accompanied her to the orientation and took notes for her.

I had changed agencies after Trudy began her greeting career at Wal-Mart, but I never stopped wondering if the job worked out. I had concerns her bus transportation may be late getting her to work. For those of us who can drive a car, we rarely know the stress of depending on another for transportation.

*Names changed to protect privacy

I was pleased two months later when Trudy called to chat. She was her same bubbly self, but had a surprising update on her job situation. Trudy had been fired! I was shocked. I thought the position of Greeter was meant for her, but I learned she had fallen asleep on the job one too many times.

For sure, the most amusing adult client I've had was 35-year-old Nixon*. His mother was a single parent and short of statue, barely five feet tall. However, Nixon had reached over six feet tall by age 15. He did fairly well caring for his personal needs such as toileting, showering, and eating. His dear mother had done a fantastic job teaching her son to be clean and have appropriate manners. We never heard what had happened to Nixon's father, but I imagine he was also a tall man.

On occasion, Nixon stayed late at my home while his mother worked. One evening at supper Nixon had enjoyed eating his hot dog with a lot of catsup and mustard. For the next three hours, he let out huge belches. The kind of noisy burp where you think, "Oh great. Get a bucket, quick!" But then to my relief, Nixon would mumble repeatedly, "Catsup and mustard, catsup and mustard. That's what it is, catsup and mustard. …"

Having spotted mail addressed to Big Nutz, Nixon felt it imperative to call my husband, Big. Being the humorous man Dan is, he often signs his name this way. So far, it's only been a problem at the bank. One teller got in deep do-do because she accepted that signature and didn't ask for his identification. They all know us though. And now, Nixon, as well, knows, Big Nutz.

*Names changed to protect privacy

As per instructions from Nixon's mother one evening, we were to make sure he showered before her return at 11:30 p.m., which was later than normal. She gave us a small suitcase with Nixon's soap, shampoo, powder, toothbrush, toothpaste, and clean clothing meticulously placed inside. Later in the evening, I led Nixon into the bathroom and unzipped his suitcase so he could easily see the needed items. After I turned the shower water on to his desired temperature, I left the room. He was instructed to call for me if he needed help.

I waited around the hall corner in our family room listening to the sound of running water. When it was shut off, I knocked quietly on the bathroom door and asked Nixon if he needed my assistance (hoping he would say no). He said he was a big boy and could dry himself off.

After 15 minutes, I figured he must be dried and dressed. I returned to the bathroom, but the door was hanging wide open. No Nixon in sight. I could tell he had used some of the items in his backpack, but his clothes were on the counter. Our children were in bed and the only opened door in the hallway was the master bedroom. I called out to Nixon and he replied with, "I'm ready, Diane!" I slowly walked toward my bedroom. A quick gaze inside and I immediately retreated. Yikes, there he was, a grown man lying buck-naked on my bed, cross-wise on top of my quilt, with his legs pointed straight up in the air! I assumed he had heard my little yelp when he repeated, "I'm ready Diane. Come powder my nuts!"

Never running across this challenge before, I hurried out to the garage and found Dan laboring to replace a car starter. I didn't tell him much besides to hurry inside, I needed his assistance. He followed me reluctantly to the bathroom, where I handed him Nixon's large container of baby powder. I pointed to our open bedroom door and said, "He's in there waiting. He needs you to powder his nuts."

"DO WHAT?" Dan replied.

"Come on, Big, you can do this!"

I led him to the door and instructed my kind-hearted husband to just run in there, cover his eyes, and quickly sprinkle the designated area with powder.

Nixon called out again, "I'm ready for you to powder my nuts, Diane!"

On the count of three, my hubby obediently followed his loving wife's instructions. Nixon returned to the bathroom once his nuts were powdered by Big Nutz and proceeded to get dressed without any other assistance. After that happened, I knew I owed Dan BIG TIME!

Unfortunate

Though most of my experiences as a respite/habilitation provider and caregiver have been positive and rewarding, there have been some difficult situations. Comparable to other families, parental figures work on different levels with a variety of styles.

I have been bitten, scratched, pinched and slugged by clients. These children with special needs get frustrated when they cannot communicate their wants and needs. A few are given special medications to help calm their behaviors. The prescribed medicines usually meet the purpose, when given correctly and consistently.

Three clients I worked with, in the past 30-plus years, had parents who thought it was in their child's best interest to take a break from the behavioral medications. Those vacations from meds times would fall on my watch. These three different sets of parents

*Names changed to protect privacy

refused to medicate their child usually on the weekends and holidays. Trying to handle the children with extreme behaviors proved unsuccessful after two or three visits in my home.

I thrive on challenges, as mentioned previously, but not at the expense of my well-being and protection of others within the walls of my home. All these clients were my size or larger. One boy slugged me in the chest so hard I almost fell over. I stood in my backyard with him, speaking softly, encouraging him to calm down. Thankfully, he only had the one outburst on his second visit to my home.

Later, this mother acknowledged her son's actions were unacceptable. I offered to work with him again, if she would administer his medication that day. She insisted her son needed a rest from his prescription. It was odd to me that this mother could not comprehend why, when I informed her that his rest would be somewhere other than in my home.

Other situations were similarly disturbing to me, when I had been bitten and hit by two other teens on vacation from behavior medications. Again, these parents were not happy campers when given notice that I would no longer be able to provide respite care for their children.

A few years ago, I had an opportunity to work with a delightful and high functioning 27-year-old named Terri*. The agency informed me Terri had several hours of respite and habilitation available. Her first visit proved she had much potential and hopefully would be able to hold a job in the future.

Her parents worked long hours and preferred that I transported Terri to and from her home. When this was not an option for me, Terri's sister-in-law, Ann*, would help transport. Ann had a pleasant attitude and told me this was not a problem, since her husband and pre-school aged child lived in the home as well.

I spent many hours working with Terri on independent living skills. It was quite apparent that Terri spent most of her time in front of the television or playing video games. She was not even skilled at completing a simple task such as washing dishes. It was not due to her lack of intelligence. It was a deficiency of experience.

The father was searching for complete transportation assistance for his daughter. He mentioned to me that he would like Terri to go to a day center program a couple of times during the week. That was a very agreeable arrangement for me. I saw great possibilities for Terri to continue as my client two to three times a week.

After almost three full weeks, Terri seemed to be smiling more. A slight air of confidence was beginning to overshadow her shy nature. I was feeling a sense of reward from the repetitive activities of teaching Terri essential life skills. I had plans to continue and implement more lessons.

One evening, I had taken Terri home. We chatted about the next day's lunch where she would work on making a grilled cheese sandwich again and that we would do kick-boxing or yoga. She said she'd see me in the morning and waved good-bye.

Later that evening, I received an email from Terri's mother. It said that Terri's father was really upset at the day program for denying Terri's admission. He called the agency in charge of the day program and respite and habilitation hours. He told them he was pulling all of Terri's hours from them. That was the end of my plans to help further Terri's knowledge of everyday chores and life-skills.

It bothered me that neither of Terri's parents called to discuss this sudden change. There was also another issue I had on my hands. Before I could fax in paperwork with my hours worked with Terri, I needed a parental signature. I arranged with Ann, Terri's sister-in-law, for me to come by their house the next evening and acquire a parent's autograph. Ann seemed to be the only person in the home willing to speak with me. She said Terri's father would be there after work.

The next morning, I spoke to the receptionist from the agency and confirmed that all of her hours had been pulled. I felt saddened that Terri wasn't allowed to be my client any longer after she had already made progress in many areas.

I decided it would be beneficial to type notes for Terri's next provider and caseworker. It may be to Terri's best interest to add some of the skills we had worked on to her habilitation goal sheet.

Once again, I was only able to speak with Ann, when I arrived at Terri's home to get a signature. Ann retreated into the home, as I stood outside. Terri came out to say hi and I told her I would miss her and that I enjoyed working with her. Here's a rough copy of the note regarding Terri's progress.

Terri :   Independent Living Skills, May–June

1. Community: ordering food, speaking up in a plain audible voice, not interrupting, making her requests appropriately, and saying thank you and such. Visiting, encouraged interacting.
2. Exercise: videos-Yoga, dance, kick-boxing, stretching. Follow cues correctly and carefully, keeping the pace up, practicing left and right directions.
3. Cooking Skills: preparing and cooking grilled cheese sandwich, clean up.
4. Cake mix: Properly, mixing and baking cake using stove timer, cleaning up dishes and putting things away in the proper place.
5. Writing/spelling skills: working on clearer writing and spelling skills to prepare to fill out a job application in the future.
6. Housecleaning, laundry: light housecleaning such as dusting, sweeping, wiping kitchen table and counters, emptying trash containers, folding laundry neatly.
7. Hygiene: brushing teeth at least for one minute, rinsing mouth and cleaning area. Applying mascara and combing hair. Washing hands when needed.
8. Grocery shopping: learning to choose the best fruits and vegetables, washing properly/drying, putting away, clean up.
9. Making jewelry: assisted Terri in creating a colorful bracelet.

I have enjoyed working with Terri the past few weeks. She is very pleasant, has great manners, strives to follow instructions and safety rules. I wish her the best in the future to reach her full potential.

I have given a few examples of some unfortunate clients whom I believe, a large part of any failures progressing in life are due to their parents' unwillingness to put their child's needs ahead of their own.

Look IN Me illustration by Angel R. Gonzalez Jr.

Not Twins

I've been a respite provider for one family for over 21 years. At first, three-year-old Aurelia* was their only child, being severely disabled since birth. This girl's smile was a mile wide and it lit up a room. A few months after I began to care for Aurelia, her baby brother, Lloyd*, while in uteri, suffered a brain hemorrhage and was taken via emergency Cesarean section one month early. The parents were given very little hope that he would survive. If he endured the many complications upon his birth, he would also be disabled physically and mentally.

Most of us will never experience such an immense challenge. I feel overwhelming stress if a child of mine is ill for a week. But I always have hope that my child will get well soon. With two children being severely disabled, your sincere desire as a parent is for the best mental and physical care to assist them in maintaining life. You hope to keep up with their ongoing needs. Your mind

*Names changed to protect privacy

becomes bogged down with future appointments your children must be brought to, including physical therapy, occupational therapy, speech therapy, wheelchair clinics, and more. The list is endless depending on your child's special needs.

After three months, Lloyd was cleared to become another respite client of mine. The doctors were amazed that he had lived through this brain trauma. His mother breast fed him with a lot of work on her part. Lloyd appeared externally normal in every way. My older children fought over who could hold him next. He would even smile at times. And his cry was loud, exceptionally normal. As this cute chubby little body grew, his disabilities became more evident.

Since Aurelia was very petite for a three-year-old, our five daughters, Rochelle, Dana, Torri, Amy and Nikki enjoyed holding and playing with her. Even more so was my older son, Chad. As soon as the family's van pulled into our driveway, Chad would yell, "I get Aurelia!" This big teenage man-child would rush out to carry Aurelia still in her car seat, into our home as she grinned ear to ear. It was endearing to Aurelia's mother, as well as to Chad's mother—me.

One year our daughters put their money together and went Christmas shopping for Aurelia and Lloyd. I hadn't noticed this much enthusiasm from my daughters before. They took immense pleasure in shopping for their special friends, buying two cute stylish outfits for both children. Then, when Aurelia and Lloyd showed up, dressed in their new clothes, my daughters were even more excited!

Having had these children in our home for so many years helped our own children gain empathy and acceptance for others they interacted with. Parents and teachers shared with us how kind our children were to a child with special needs, or someone different with problems. This is one benefit of my job, and it has become more rewarding as a result.

In the beginning, Aurelia and Lloyd were small enough to sit in child car seats in my vehicle. It was quite a task, however, to lift the two heavy seats into my van and fasten them securely, in the summer heat six months out of the year. Yes, living in Arizona, leaving the cool house and loading the car is like jumping into a toaster oven, until the air conditioning circulates. I felt great appreciation and relief when their mother arrived to fetch her precious special children.

We observed that Aurelia was more aware of her surroundings and understood conversations. Lloyd was always more into the bodily noises that cause the male species to snicker. Whenever our son, Speedy, would rail out his unusually lengthy thunderous burps, Lloyd would bust up with laughter! It was quite amusing. Even when Lloyd was 21 years old, he got the biggest kick out of those sounds, as well as sounds of something hitting the floor, or someone passing gas—the usual silly resonances in life.

When our friends would meet the brother and sister I cared for, many of them would ask if they were twins. When Aurelia's hair was cut short, she looked a lot like her brother.

Eventually both children became unable to tolerate oral feedings. Each had a gastric button surgically placed, allowing them to be tube-fed with a special nutritional formula for the rest of their lives.

Before this surgical procedure, we endured many bouts of both children throwing up. One evening I was feeding Aurelia, as I held her, supporting her head, while slowly spooning small bites of mashed Spaghetti-os into her mouth. My daughter, Amy, was doing her homework while observing me. Aurelia smiled at Amy, then leisurely turned her head back in my direction and heaved, in my face! It was like a scene from the movie, *The Exorcist*. I was a mess. Aurelia was a mess. Amy's eyes widened and she was speechless (which was unusual), waiting for my reaction. Calmly as I was able, I cleaned up the two of us and changed Aurelia into fresh clothing. I announced to Amy, "I'm going to take a quick shower now. Give me a holler if Aurelia needs anything." While showering, I actually cried with frustration. *Why, oh why, was I in this line of work?* I regained my composure after my short meltdown. And once again, my empathy increased for the parents of these unique children.

Both children, Aurelia and Lloyd, are now adults in their 20's and heavier to lift. Both have undergone major surgeries to support internal organs that were under pressure from misshaped bones and underused muscles. The atrophy brought on by sitting in a wheelchair has increased the difficulty of lifting the children.

Their mother is a super-lady to me. Her husband is now physically disabled as well. Their local church group along with an auto agency was generous enough to contribute a van that transports three wheelchairs. This one lady cares for three family members, with minimal assistance, who relies on her physical and emotional strength. Her responsibilities are ongoing, 24 hours a day, every day. She doesn't get much time-off and suffers from migraines. Whenever I long for a vacation, I think of Aurelia's and Lloyd's mother and father who will get very little, if any, vacation time. Thankfully, the state agencies are given monies to provide such families respite services and attendant care, which is about 60 hours a month per disabled individual.

When I interviewed their mother, I inquired further of her children's diagnoses. The findings for Aurelia were far-sighted, scoliosis, along with several motor control conditions. Her records list these things as asymmetrical schizencephaly from a bleed in the brain before birth, causing cerebral palsy. Lloyd's diagnoses included a bleed in the brain toward the end of the second trimester, causing hydrocephalus and cerebral palsy. He had scoliosis and was far-sighted as well.

This mother stated at times she's very concerned if others consider her children a burden to society or should have never been born. As her mind wonders toward this negativity, inevitably, some total stranger approaches and happily interacts with one of the children. People, who meet her offspring, remember and adore them years down the road. This wonderful type of encounter snaps her back to the reality that her children are important and do contribute to society in their own magical way.

Parents in this situation with children who age, but never will become self-sufficient adults are required to petition the court for legal guardianship when the child(ren) turn 18 years of age. If you are lucky enough to find an attorney willing to take on the case pro bono, you may not have to pay as much money filing (1" thick stack of paperwork) and going to court. Yes, you must take your child or children at age 18 to court. The judge will rule if your adult child is unable to care for themselves. The fee could be around 800 dollars per child.

Aurelia at her high school graduation

Aurelia and grandson Noah

Buddies Janel and Aurelia

Lloyd has since passed away

Heavenly Laughter

News on June 20 that Lloyd had passed away peacefully in his home at age 21, left me in a sad state. I had cared for him one week previously, and all seemed well. My husband, Dan, was asked to speak at the services. Our son, Speedy, would be accompanying Lloyd's uncle, with a special musical number.

I went to visit the family the day after Lloyd's passing. I was particularly concerned as to how Aurelia was doing. She has never experienced a close loved one's death. It's also unclear of her comprehension of such an event. She smiled as I hugged her and complimented her on her pretty outfit. The father and mother were having a difficult time keeping their composure, but we all tried our best to not upset Aurelia.

The next week was the viewing and funeral services of our buddy, Lloyd. His still body seemed very much at peace. I believe he is overjoyed now and desires his family know of his happiness. His parents seem to be coping as well as can be expected. They have much support from family, friends, and fellow church members.

Dan was the first to speak at the memorial services. His talk went something like this:

My wife, Diane, began caring for Aurelia and Lloyd over 21 years ago. Our teenagers looked forward to the van pulling into our driveway. After the birth of Lloyd, I remember our daughter, Amy, yelling out, "I get Lloyd!" First one to the van carried in Lloyd usually. The next teen out gladly carted in Aurelia. I was just an innocent bystander, but over the next 21 years I came to know and love these two children, as did my whole family.

Now before I go any further, I ought to point out that Lloyd's family are Mormons. I am a Mormon. We are gathered here in a Mormon Church. I suspect most everybody here are Mormons. If you are not, I should warn you that I am about to start sounding like a Mormon. If I should say something that you don't understand, just make a note and ask someone later.

You see, there are some outside of our faith, and even some in our faith, who allow the existence of children like Lloyd to shake their faith. They ask, how can a just and loving God allow children to go through life like this?

In the L.D.S. Family Proclamation, third paragraph we read, "In the premortal realm, spirit sons and daughters knew and worshipped God as their Eternal Father and accepted His plan by which His children could obtain a physical body and gain earthly experience to progress toward perfection and ultimately realize their divine destiny as heirs of eternal life."

I believe Lloyd, like the rest of us, was there. He accepted the Lord's plan. He received a physical body, and gained earthly experience. His mortal experience was not the same as our mortal experience, but it was still a mortal experience. After all, life is a carnival. At the carnival, there are rides to be ridden, games to be played, shows to be seen, and food to be eaten. Lloyd might not have attended the same carnival as us, but it was still a carnival and it was wonderful. He experienced life. He felt hot and cold, saw lights and colors, heard sounds, tasted food, smelled smells and enjoyed the ride. He felt joy and pain.

I've had many conversations with Lloyd. I would like to share four observations about Lloyd.

1. *Lloyd had a sense of awe and wonder. He loved taking in the sights of lights and color. He would stare at Christmas trees, the television, and other bright things. He especially enjoyed different sounds. I would go out to the garage and bring in copper tubes, an old cymbal, and a harmonica, anything I could find that would make a noise and hold it close to his ear and watch his eyes light up as he tried to process new sounds.*

2. *Lloyd had a wonderful sense of humor, which was a wild curiosity to me. We never knew what he was going to find funny. One day I dropped a fork in the kitchen and heard Lloyd laughing in the living room. Now I'm in the kitchen throwing silverware on the floor, and Lloyd is in the other room splitting a gut, laughing hysterically! Finally, Diane had to come in and tell me to stop. Being a typical little boy, Lloyd was particularly fond of bodily noises. So, I found him a toy. It's your standard fart machine* (demonstration). *I was worried that I would abuse this toy until, someday, Diane might hide it from me. I was wrong. I came home and found that she had placed it near Lloyd and was*

carrying the remote around with her, lighting it off often for his amusement (another demonstration). *Lloyd loved the sound of a good fart (*an arm to lip demonstration*). Now, let's all get our arms out and let one off for Lloyd. All together now, one, two...* (Group fart sound effect). *If you listen carefully, you can almost hear Lloyd laughing. Lloyd also enjoyed a good belch. Our son Speedy was especially skilled at this. Speedy could roar like a lion. Speedy, would you please?* (Speedy, who is seated on the stand, belches.) *Lloyd loved that. As Lloyd got older, he recognized things out of the ordinary. He would find humor anywhere. One occasion Diane came walking through the living room backwards. Lloyd found that to be hilarious. Now Diane was marching backwards around Lloyd chanting nonsense for his amusement. Oh, Lloyd's laughter really was intoxicating.*

3. *Lloyd was a brave soul. It's hard to explain this, but he was bent and obviously uncomfortable much of the time. Yet he took it with a quiet dignity, and didn't complain much. He was just a brave, little soul.*

4. *Lloyd was fearless. He simply lacked fear. Loud sudden noises, like thunder, fireworks, the crashing of a vase, he just found amusing. You could get in his face and shout, and he'd laugh. One of my great pleasures was taking Lloyd out to the van when it was time to go home. We would go past their van and sprint donuts in the street. I would run him in his wheelchair up and down the street and spin him around in circles, and he couldn't get enough. I tried spinning Aurelia, but could clearly see she was nervous. Not Lloyd. He loved it! His smile was a ray of sunshine. His laughter was music to us.*

Now, I'm gonna tell ya what I really think. I believe Lloyd was a valiant warrior in the pre-existence. The proclamation says we accepted the Lord's plan. Lloyd didn't merely accept it, but fought bravely for the Lord and His Plan of Redemption. I believe Lloyd fearlessly denounced that fraud and glory-seeker Lucifer and his plan that held no merit and no guarantee other than his weak claim that he would do it.

I had a sacred, personal experience once. I've always believed that sacred personal experiences should be kept both sacred, and personal. But because of where we are today, I think I'd like to share this with you.

I had a dream a couple of years ago, in which I saw a glimpse of resurrection morning. In my dream, I saw the Savior take the hand of a child like unto Lloyd and raise him up. He stood straight, whole, and amazingly handsome. He looked like a returned missionary. This child like unto Lloyd, now a man, looked up, and saw that he was in the presence of the Son of God. He immediately dropped to one knee. The Lord then reached down a second time and took this child like unto Lloyd and raised him up again. This time the two of them looked into each other's eyes, and they both grinned. This is when I awoke. But it was in that grin that I understood. I saw recognition. Oh, my goodness, these two knew each other on a personal level. These two were friends in that former life.

I hope I didn't go too far with this, but that's what I think. Perhaps that explains why the Lord chose this path for Lloyd. Lloyd was placed outside of Satan's reach. The devil would have no influence on him, couldn't touch him.

In closing, I would like to thank Lloyd's parents for allowing me this chance of sharing my feelings about their son. And thank you for allowing us to have your son in our home so many times over the last 21 years. His smile was a ray of sunshine. His laughter was music.

Larry in Glacier Park

Dan tells a story from his past:

Being married to Diane, my life has been filled with experiences among people with special needs. Looking back, I think my favorite encounter was before I met Diane, while driving a tour bus in Glacier National Park, in the summer of 1975.

It was a pleasant day. I was parked in front of the East Glacier Park Lodge, collecting tickets and greeting passengers. In line I saw them, an elderly couple with a full-grown son who stood out as being mentally challenged.

The couple introduced me to Larry*, who was wearing bright summer clothes, and a straw hat. Larry immediately announced he wanted to see a bear and a moose. I warned him that I could not promise either. The wild is quite different from a zoo. He also informed me that he had his swim trunks on under his shorts and was hoping that we would stop at a lake so he could go swimming. I gently explained that we would drive by several lakes, but would

*Names changed to protect privacy

not have time to stop and swim in any of them. Larry was quite disappointed. I further explained that at this altitude, the water in the lake is from melting snow and very very cold. This only made matters worse. Larry had his heart set on swimming. He was wearing his swim trunks after all. Larry simply believed I was trying to interfere with his summer vacation plans.

Once the passengers were seated and it was time to go, I launched into my routine. I introduced myself, and allowed the usual moment for everyone to chuckle at my last name. I then explained the route we would take, and what we would see along the way. As I surveyed my group, I noticed Larry and his parents sat in the back row, and Larry was glaring at me. If we were not stopping to swim in any lake, then he was not going to be happy.

The tour began with some interesting facts about the East Glacier Park Hotel, including the size, construction and age of the beautiful facility. From the back of the bus I heard someone mutter, "Bullshit." There was a quiet moment of stunned surprise. Apparently, we had a disgruntled passenger on board. Continuing on with a brief history of the park also brought a similar response, "Bullshit." By now everyone on the bus was becoming familiar with Larry.

Soon another passenger seated near Larry and his parents was encouraging him on. While naming mountains along the trip, this new friend would whisper, "Sounds like bullshit, huh, Larry?"

By the time we reached our destination, everyone on the bus was calling out, "Bullshit" in unison to everything I said and laughing. It could not have been any better!

That was 41 years ago, but I still remember the fun those people had on my "Bullshit" tour with a little help from Larry, who was no longer mad. Indeed, Larry thoroughly enjoyed being the center of attention.

As everyone filed off the bus, I received big surprise that day, money. And lots of it! Tips were not uncommon, but this was a record breaking day for me. And that ain't no bullshit!

-Told by Dan

Peacekeeper

Told by Kathy:

I have a beautiful sister named Amy Elizabeth. She was born with Down syndrome in 1967. She is loving, gentle, kind, funny, loves to tease, and loves her family with all her heart.

About 30 years ago, things were extra tight financially for me. My marriage was falling apart and it was Christmas. I didn't know what we were going to be able to do for the girls that year. I was over at my parents' home discussing the problem with my mother. I remember crying because I felt so helpless.

At that time, Amy folded towels for a junior high school in Twin Falls, Idaho. She was paid 25 cents per towel. It wasn't very much money. On this particular day, Amy was in her room listening to music. But she came into the living room with my mother and me.

She had a stack of paper in her hands, which she handed to me saying, "Here sister. For Kari and the twins." Most of the checks only amounted to two to three dollars, but she handed them all to me. The checks totalled about 15 dollars, certainly not enough to take care of Christmas. But Amy had succeeded in lifting my spirits with her generous gift.

I know without a doubt, that those born like Amy are certainly God's most perfect spirits. She continues to bless our family every day.
                                        -Kathy

Photos provided by Kathy

Amy

Poem to Amy Elizabeth:

A Mother's Journey to Love

Women have a strong inner strength, I often boast
However, when things happen to those that we love the most
It sometimes shakes us to our very core as we feel the scathe
So often these are times that develop "Women of Faith"
This happened to me in nineteen hundred and sixty-seven
Months in bed...then a very special delivery from Heaven
This little bundle was Amy Elizabeth by name
Five daughters were now our biggest claim to fame
Instead of being happy, I felt strangely numb
As I was told my baby daughter had Down syndrome
Totally shocked, and asking so often, "Why me...Why me?"
My heart felt broken, how could I ever again be happy?
My husband wisely counselled in a gently way
"Why not you Earline...things will be okay"
I struggled along for probably a month or two
Then I began to pull myself together, as women so often do
I again began to smell the roses; my heart was filled with love
I realized this child of mine was a gift from God above
Blessed are the peacemakers, the beatitude made for her
A priceless gift even better than gold, frankincense, or myrrh
Hospital stays were frequent in her first nine years
Many close calls, and may I add...many tears
Our whole family applauded each new task she learned to do
And tears came to my eyes when she first said, "I love you"
She's nearly thirty-two and apparently having too much fun

As the doctors told us she would be lucky to reach the age of one
At four feet eleven, she's not very tall
We like to think of her as our little doll
She has taught our family to be more patient, loving, and kind
Are these some of the blessings God had in mind?
We can't see the blessings when we are sad
Wondering how God could let things get so bad
God not giving us more than we can handle is true
When we do our best He will carry us through
Of this I can testify as my life continues to unfold
And as I tell my story that until now was untold
That we may all be "Women of Faith" I pray
Able to face each year, each month, each week, each day
Life isn't always easy, sometimes we stumble and fall
Staying close to the Lord makes the journey worth it all

-Earline, Amy's mother (1999)

Amy

Amy

There was a small child born.

Some did deride and hold her in scorn.

True, from the cup of knowledge she had but a sip,

But never a mean word passed her lip.

While others gained knowledge and fame,

She had to work hard to write her name.

She would never reach great worldly heights,

But she learned to put greater things in her sight.

While others would push and shove and puff up in pride,

Never did she seek reasons to deride.

She sought not earthly skills,

But drank from loftier wells.

From the pools of love, kindness, humor and charity,

From these she would see life in true clarity.

She became loved by all that met her,

And for the Lord, and us, a beloved daughter.

-Terry, Amy's father

Puzzling Indeed

I met a family through an agency that hired me to do respite, as I had many other families. These parents had adopted two sons from Korea and after fostering a girl with special needs, adopted her as well. Even though Susan was born blind, her brothers managed to teach her to do puzzles. They also helped her memorize the capitals of every state.

A friend of ours, being a scout leader, was looking for an experience with individuals with special needs, for the older boys in scouts, ages 15 to 18. I knew they would be totally amazed at Susan's ability to blindly piece a puzzle together.

Five scouts were seated with Susan at my kitchen table. I had six different 50-piece puzzles of animals. Each was cut into 50 pieces, with similar sizes. I explained that since Susan was blind, the boys would all need to blindfold their eyes with the cloth placed at their seats.

Most of the boys were very determined, and since Susan had a very low I.Q. they thought this game wouldn't be much of a challenge. But after 15 minutes of struggling to fit the puzzle pieces together, only one boy had found two pieces that would work. On the other side of the table, however, Susan had fit together almost half of the puzzle! After 25 minutes three of the boys had given up and were putting their puzzle together without their blindfolds. Susan finished first and giggled when she heard none of these boys was triumphant.

The scouts learned a valuable lesson that day. There are special people in the world gifted in different areas of life skills that they (the boys) may never master. I think it is a gift from God to understand how every individual is unique in some way, even if they have disabilities.

From Susan's mother:

When Susan was adopted at age five, she was unable to speak. Every night before bedtime, I would place Susan on her father's lap. He'd place his large manly hands on Susan's adorable face and tell her, "Daddy loves you."

Susan, being blind since birth, would never be able to identify anyone by sight. We, as her loving parents, were helping her recognize voices and physical contact. Night after night, Susan would sit on her daddy's lap and hear him say that he loved her. She did not speak a word for months. Then one evening, after her father told her yet again, "Daddy loves you," Susan put her hands on his face and repeated, "Daddy loves you."

She has two brothers, John and Jaime. The oldest brother, John, is three years older than Susan. She is especially close to her brother, Jaime, because he's only a few months younger than her. Jaime loved to rough-house with Susan. She would howl with laughter at his gentle bantering. It was quite comical to watch these two siblings wrestling become the best of friends.

A few years went by and Jaime was ready to move out. His new residence was not close by. We explained to Susan ahead of time what was about to happen. We tried our best to prepare her. However, the week that Jaime had moved out, Susan was very upset and would cry every day. I attempted to calm and reassure her. Since her vocabulary had increased dramatically, Susan would even talk to Jaime on the phone. She was still extremely difficult to console. Finally, I asked her why she missed her brother so badly. Susan exclaimed to me, "I just need a good body slam!"

-Jackie

No Difference

David was the second child born to Tim and Arely. After having one healthy baby, they hadn't expected anything different. David was that *different* they hadn't anticipated. This took place years ago before modern medicine could predict various birth defects.

I became David's respite provider when he was 15 years old. He was an interesting guy; blind, non-verbal, diapered, and somewhat ambulatory. David towered over many at six feet and one inch. He had a lean body and not much muscle tone. He was easygoing and wore a huge grin most of the day.

The elementary school took advantage of David's musical abilities. He could clap to any beat of music. The band director usually sat David front and center, seated beside a drum. The joy on David's face captured the audience's attention from the beginning of the concert. David contentedly pounded on the drum with perfect timing.

If you've ever wondered how children with special needs are integrated into a normal functioning classroom, David, using his musical talents, would be explanation enough. This gives the rest of the student body experience with others born unique. I became aware that if a child discriminates against another child, it is a learned behavior. Most likely an adult has shown (taught) the child to be intolerant.

Many years ago, as I was a young mother of four children, I was discussing with my kindergartner, about a friend she had met in her classroom. My daughter, Torri, knew the hair color of her friend and what color of dress this friend had worn. When I asked the adult question, "Did she have brown skin?" Torri seemed confused. She really hadn't noticed anyone in her classroom with different colored skin. Torri totally accepted all her classmates as her equal. This was an eye-opener. My daughter had humbled me.

Most of my children grew up around children with special needs visiting our home, sometimes daily. Now, as adults, my children are compassionate, unbiased grown-ups, showing kindness to all. I've often thought if all humans were given the experience of actively associating with individuals with special needs from an early age, that we would be more like my daughter was in kindergarten. We'd accept all as our equal, as well as feeling at ease with those with differences.

Having a mind of his own, David decides when he's finished eating or drinking. He will hold the liquid or food in his mouth refusing to swallow. One day I was about to feed him enchiladas but happened to notice something in his mouth already. It was a grape! He had been in our home almost two hours and we didn't have any grapes. I knew it was left over from a snack he was given in his home. Your guess is as good as mine as to how long he held that grape in his mouth.

David has been an unofficial member of our family now for over 18 years. He is just one of many. He amazes us, as his senses of smell and hearing seem to be amplified. Whenever I feed him, bringing a spoon toward his mouth, it flies open! Being blind seems to intensify his other senses.

From David's mother:

When David was born he seemed to be completely normal. At the time, photographers would come to the hospital to make appointments to come to your house to take pictures once the baby was lifting his head.

A couple of months later, photographers started calling to see if David was lifting his head. I finally said yes, even though he was not. They came to our house and started taking pictures, but before the photographer left he said, "I have taken a lot of baby pictures and I have never seen a baby with despondent eyes such as his."

I had already noticed that David did not look at me. I expressed my concern to the pediatrician. He told me some babies develop their sight late. After the photographer made the comment, I took David to a child ophthalmologist and he verified my worst fears. My baby was blind.

When David was four months old, we took him to the pediatrician once again. He panicked because David was not lifting his head. He referred us to the UCLA hospital where several tests were done. The results confirmed David had cerebral palsy and was completely blind.

For years after, I'd cry, but finally came to accept David's disabilities and I have moved on. I know now that Heavenly Father sent him to us for a reason.

It is so rewarding to see David always happy no matter what goes on around him. One Sunday at church I brought him to Primary (ages three-12 years old) to do a show-and-tell. This was to teach the children about disabled individuals. I pointed out how fortunate we are to be healthy. I told the children that we should be thankful we can see, speak and walk...I also taught the Primary children not to be afraid of people who have disabilities.

One of the most challenging things about David would be his inability to talk to us when something is wrong. I wish I could sense his needs ahead of time. Even with that trial, we are very thankful to have David and we would not have it any other way.

-Arely

Less than one week after my interview with Arely, routine blood work revealed that David's kidneys were shutting down. Tim, David's father related to me that he and his wife had a goal since David was born. They hoped to outlive David to be able to care for him his entire life. Looks like their prayer was answered. Doctors could not predict how much time David had to live. Hospice was called in to help in keeping him comfortable. Dan and I recently went to visit with David one final time. It was very emotional for me. I gave David one last hug and whispered in his ear, "Remember me, David." The time many of us had with David is quite a bit longer than envisioned when he was an infant. We will always be Nutz about David!

David passed away in his home, peacefully, February 2017

David was always a happy guy. His favorite position was lying down with his feet up in the air as if he was "Dancin' on the Ceiling".

Unseen Vision

Not much hope was given to parents of a premature baby years ago. Jared was born with cataracts, leukemia and other health concerns. By the time he hit age seven, there was no trace of leukemia. Now, at age 43, Jared has lived with severe visual impairment his entire life. This resulted in his most prevalent challenge in life: not being able to drive.

Jared stated, "I like cars even though I can't drive them, especially cars from the 1920's to the 1980's. Cars from these decades are my favorite because they're a symbol of a simpler time. It's the era when people actually worked on the assembly lines in the factories building our automobiles by hand, instead of having robots doing the job like they do nowadays."

Jared was in special education classes because of learning disabilities until high school when he was integrated into a regular American History course. During his junior year Jared took a radio broadcasting class at a technology school. He was unable to get into the broadcasting profession as a disc jockey because it was too competitive. Being a social guy, Jared's never had difficulty making friends. This is very rewarding to him. He mentioned to me that most people he's met are very helpful.

As I interviewed Jared, I was thinking, *I wish I had his amazing memory of dates!* He remembers many exact dates of things such as the numerous surgeries he's had, which include right and left eye muscle repair (1980), testicular cancer (2006), right eye cornea transplant (2012), left eye cornea transplant (2013), second cornea transplant on left eye because the first donor wasn't a good match (2013), a tube shunt placed in his right eye to drain the fluid, due to glaucoma, to keep the pressure down (2016). He also recalls the dates of certain television shows, sporting events, and music, even those that happened before his birth.

In 1979, while Jared attended The Foundation for Blind Children, the teachers took the students bowling now and then. And so began Jared's love for bowling at age five. When he found out about Special Olympics bowling in 2004, his talent for the sport flourished.

From 2000 to 2006 Jared worked as a respite provider for a relative of his. When he received the diagnosis of testicular cancer, he gave the agency notice regarding how much time he might need off work for surgery and radiation treatment. About three weeks later he received a termination notice from the agency. Even though Jared was surprised by the letter, he didn't follow through with recourse, as he had planned on searching for a different job soon.

One old television show Jared enjoys watching is *Hee Haw*. Being an avid reader, Jared recalls many facts. He is the fondest of reading westerns by Louis L'Amour. Going along with a western theme, Jared loves country music. Being able to name the artist of old or new country will amaze any avid listener. However, classic rock rates highest as his favorite genre. He would have fit right in with my teenage crowd in the 70's!

With enthusiasm Jared mentions, "I like watching the Phoenix Suns basketball games! I turn the sound down on my TV set and turn the radio on to the Suns play-by-play announcer Al McCoy. I enjoy listening to him. He's been broadcasting the Suns games for 45 years, since 1972. With my vision impairment, that's how I follow their games."

Finding value in humor is of great worth to Jared. Even though his parents had divorced many years previously, Jared's life amplifies the positive qualities his father had including finding humor. Jared's father was his biggest fan for sure. It was 2014 when his father passed away. In the early 80's his family lived on a cul-de-sac in Phoenix. Jared recalls with a grin how his father would turn off the engine a few houses from theirs, and coast into the driveway. It made him howl with laughter seeing how far the car would travel without power. To this day, Jared will retell this story to someone transporting him and dare them to try it. This never fails to bring hilarity to all passengers in the vehicle.

His step-father treats Jared and his four siblings as if they were his biological children, which means a lot to them. Jared's mother and step-father have influenced his life immensely. They give him confidence that he can do anything, even though he's visually impaired.

Present day goals for Jared include graduating college to work as a special education assistant in high school. He also speaks of finding his sweetheart and getting married. Having lived through many miraculous healings, I have no doubt Jared has the perseverance and positive motivation to reach the stars if he so desires.

Photo provided by Jared

"It isn't as bad as you sometimes think it is. It all works out. Don't worry. I say that to myself every morning. It will all work out. Put your trust in God, and move forward with faith and confidence in the future. ..."[1]

-Gordon B. Hinckley

NOTE

1. Ensign February 2006 "Put Your Trust in God," from the funeral program for Marjorie Pay Hinkley, April 10, 2004; see also "Latter-day Counsel," Ensign October 2000, page 73

Fair Judgment

There is nothing more precious than a newborn baby, completely innocent, and the newborn scent is like none other. I believe this must be the most extraordinary occurrence on earth. Any child, no matter their appearance, is a gift from God.

As a healthy child grows, he/she learns behaviors from those they associate with as well as their environment. This is extremely complex as personalities vary and environmental effects are different from person to person.

I mentioned earlier that my five-year-old daughter, Torri, had not learned how others may judge people by their different skin tones. She saw all children in her class as equals in every sense. I told her that even though people have various colors of skin, she was correct to see them as equals.

I have observed that the more severe a child's disability, the more open and non-judgmental they are with others they meet. They do not possess the mentality to discriminate. They may be more extraordinary than we realize. Does this attribute they possess make *us* the disabled individual?

We are all unique. It's an astonishing fact that of the billions of people born on this earth, no two people are identical to another. In single births, identical twins usually have the same DNA, but still differ in personalities and such.

Most of my clients have possessed the quality of acceptance. They do not care what clothes I wear, how rich or poor I may be, or if I'm having a bad hair day. I sense their love and joy (most of the time) when I dance around or sing. Even acting goofy is fine. I feel accepted for *who* I am. There seems to be a lot we can learn from the child or adult who is disabled, including acceptance and tolerance.

5

Silent Incredibles

There are superheroes among us, unrecognizable, because they exist quietly in the shadows.

Life x 4

We've all faced trials in our lives. At these times, we reach our max and hold on for dear life. We wonder how we will bear our burdens, wishing for time to pass quickly, hoping for relief.

I've worked for the Alda* family over nine years. They've inspired me to be a better person and to be grateful for what I've been given. The pressures in my life seem trivial compared to theirs. Over 18 years ago their quadruplets were born much earlier than scheduled. The mother was very ill and it was imperative to take the babies to save her life. Their older child, Jason*, was under two years of age. He became a big brother much sooner than expected. They were here, ready or not, quadruplets; two girls, two boys, premature, underweight, and not expected to survive.

*Names changed to protect privacy

176

I made bibs for the quads before they were born. Eight years later I became their caregiver or respite provider. The parents told me of their many hospital visits and the surgeries required in those first years. I had missed their most complex stages. Their four children were severely mentally and physically delayed, diagnosed with cerebral palsy, and each in a wheelchair. Three will be tube-fed their entire life. The fourth learned to take a bottle, since he kept pulling out his button that allowed nutritional feedings. Every day brought new challenges to this family.

I'll call the quads Corey*, Rick*, Sara*, and Sidney*. I had never fathomed that any parent would be proficient enough to give complete care to four children with severe disabilities.

*Names changed to protect privacy

This mother had some regrets as to why she had chosen to go into the nursing field after Jason was born. Then the quads were born with so many medical needs. She never questioned her choice of careers after that. Her knowledge gave her the tools and confidence to provide for her children's ongoing needs.

This family not only does well, but their lives are filled with more activities than most as the parents give new meaning to *rolling with the punches*. Both parents have full-time jobs. The Aldas are quiet about their problems and show that choices define them, not circumstances. They are humble and do not expect any sympathy. Each child is loved unconditionally by their parents, and it especially touches my heart when the father plays with his daughters. They smile like any girl would, knowing their daddy loves them. No words are spoken from his girls, none are needed. Giggles and smiles tell the story.

Older brother, Jason, has a different life than most boys, having four siblings with severe disabilities. His parents have never put huge responsibilities upon him in helping care for his four siblings with disabilities. I've never seen Jason diaper or dress them. I'm sure he helped at times, but he was their brother, not their caregiver. He seems to be a laid-back kind of guy who loves motorcycle riding with both of his parents, as well as being on his high school swim team. He often takes vacations with his parents.

Each of the quads possesses a unique personality. Corey and Sara can scoot around. Rick and Sidney spend their days and nights lying or sitting in a wheelchair. Sidney recognizes familiar faces, and her smile spreads from ear to ear. Rick is usually more difficult to read, but he will let you know if he's uncomfortable. A few years back my husband, Dan, dreamed about Rick. He related that it seemed very real. Rick was standing with his Savior and introduced Dan to Him as his friend. Dan has felt a close connection to Rick since that dream.

Curly-haired Sara can be extremely moody. There's no hesitation on her part to let you know if she's displeased about something. She has managed to completely pull the button from her stomach four times on my watch while I was feeding her via gastro tube. Knowing how to knock you off your guard, she is no different than other teenage girls. I've become more at ease on proper procedure to replace it, as she fights me. I love this gal's spirit of enthusiasm!

Sara can point to her different body parts on cue. You'd be amazed as she rarely gives eye contact. Instruct her to touch her eyes, ears, nose, mouth, toes, elbow, knee and hair—and if she's in the mood, she will. Looking at books with others is one of her

179

pleasures. Watch out for those fingers however. She can grab hair or skin in an instant and boy, does it hurt! Normally Sara's a cuddle bug and thrives on hugs and attention.

The most entertaining and busy of the group is Corey. He pulls himself to a bent standing position whenever he desires. He has broken many light switches by flipping them up and down, hundreds of times with his quick fingers. Corey has acquired some vocabulary. "Bottle" and "hungry" are very useful words for him, letting caregivers know when it's his mealtime. He says "Good bye" sometimes appropriately. Corey used to say "Why?" a lot. I would answer him, "Because Diane says." He associated that with me and I became known as *Dianesays*. I absolutely love it when Corey calls out my name in that manner.

Late one evening, after all the kids had been put into bed, I crept quietly into the darkened room to place some clean folded clothes in their drawers. As I tip-toed out, Corey quietly whispered, "Dianesays." Teary eyed, I gave my buddy Corey a hug.

As you may guess, there's never a dull moment while Corey is awake. He is constantly busy, and it is challenging to provide him with safe activities. His parents spend a lot more money on toys than other parents. Corey's favorite toys talk, make music, and light up. He will stare at it, as he drools all over it, pounds on it, throws it around and basically destroys it, as he's having the time of his life. It wouldn't be fair for the parents to collect on any toy guarantees. No toy has ever passed the *Corey test*.

Corey is easily amused and intellectually stimulated by music. He sometimes mimics the tune, having autistic tendencies. I have often wondered what musical instrument Corey would have learned, because I know he possesses musical talents, even now.

One evening, as I sang "Twinkle Twinkle Little Star" to him, he figured out in one try, how to play the exact notes of that song on his mangled keyboard. We did that five times. Then he was bored with my voice, I suppose, and moved on to his original composition.

When all else fails with Corey, I will wrestle with him or give him a horsey ride. He rough-houses by slugging me. Good thing I don't return that sweet gesture of play. I doubt he would be hurt though. He is a tough 18-year-old dude. Glad he's not the size of an average teenager, or I would be in a world of hurt!

The mother of these five children is an excellent organizer. They manage to go on vacations throughout the year. To any outside person, it would seem hopeless to vacation without their quadruplets, or even *with* them. Often the parents have two to three providers to assist the family. The two grandmothers also help when possible. Relatives will take the night shift while the parents and Jason are out of town.

The quads have been in special education classes at school since age three. School is a life-saver for this family (until the quads get sick). If neighbors are in a hurry, know from experience not to drive by this family's home during bus pick up or drop off hours. Two of the quads ride on bus #1, and the other two are transported on bus #2. After sitting and waiting in their vehicle for four children to be brought into or from the house, drivers who are unfamiliar with this neighborhood, most likely think this house is a group home.

My experience working for this amazing family will forever be etched in my mind. I'm not sure if I would be able to live such a *normal* life raising one child with multiple disabilities, let alone four. The parents work hard, but they manage to play hard as well.

Interviewing the father:

This family of seven consists of quadruplets born with severe disabilities over 18 years ago and an older son, age 20, who is serving a Latter-day Saint (Mormon) church mission.

The father recently related to me this fun story of when he visited the quads' special education class at the high school.

Fortunately for his son, Corey, one of the quads, the teachers arranged to have a keyboard in the classroom. Corey excitedly entertains himself by pounding on this musical instrument. He plays the same set of notes, over and over again, and tries to match the sounds while humming to himself.

The nurse tried to convey a message to a teacher while Corey hummed along, delighting himself on the keyboard. The nurse got a bit annoyed with Corey's repetitive notes and told him, "Corey, please play a different chord!" Astoundingly, Corey replied in his manly voice, "Different chord." And he immediately changed chords. His teachers are starting to comprehend that this unique child is indeed smarter than they give him credit for.

Alda Family recently

Interviewing the mother:

1. What has been one of your most difficult challenges?

One of my most difficult challenges has been family unity. Family unity is created when you work, serve, learn, and play together. We are able to do this, but in a very limited way. I've felt like a split family a lot. We needed to feel unity with our typical child and that meant doing things that the quadruplets couldn't do. On the other hand, spending time with the quads was rarely enjoyable for a teenage boy. Trying to create unity can be difficult for a family with most of the members being significantly disabled.

2. Give one example of how this has impacted your life goals.

One of my goals was motherhood, to be the best mother I could be and to love it. I am still a mother, but my role as mother is different than what I expected. I wanted to explore and learn together as a family. I was capable to do some of this with my oldest typical child for which I am grateful. However, with the quadruplets, I have been more of a caregiver. It has been a challenge at times to

183

feel joy in the quads' intellectual, emotional, and physical growth since it has been restricted by their disabilities. However, the quads have found joy in small and simple ways and so have we as parents.

3. Tell me something you have learned from your experience?

Patience, perspective, persistence, and to accept my best efforts and to be content with that.

4. What has been your biggest reward in this life-changing matter?

I believe that the biggest reward will be when they are healed and whole after this earth life. I believe that when we die, we will have the opportunity to be perfected and have a perfect body. My greatest reward will be seeing four of my children without disability and to be able to walk and talk together. However, during our lifetime, my biggest reward for this life of disability is to see my children smile because they are happy or have learned something new. Joy in life can be found by anyone.

5. Looking back on your life when things changed drastically, is there anything you would have done differently when this first occurred?

As I think back, I have concluded that I would not have done anything differently. I feel that through my education and employment as a nurse I was already familiar with the healthcare setting and had the ability to give medical care. My husband was educated and had a good job to help provide for our family. We were financially stable at that point in our life. We had recently moved close to family and had their support as well as from our church family.

6. What is the most appreciated way someone has helped you deal with this challenge?

I could think of numerous people over the years, but really, the one that stands out the most is God. He knows all my personal and family struggles. He has strengthened me in time of need. He has brought peace and comfort to my soul during the particularly hard times. He has inspired me in how to move forward. I could not have done what I have done without His help.

Photos provided by the parents

Sisterly love

A handful of 5

Corey and Sara

Sara being mischievous

Sidney

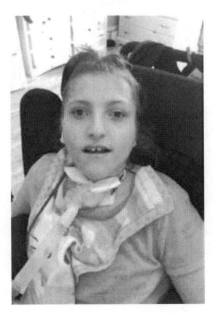

Rick

Corey composing

Corey's keyboard after two months, fit for a haunted house

Quads livin it up

A Very Special Child

In the mother's words:

As a parent of a child with special needs, I am often asked if it is hard to take care of my child, or they may say, "That must be really hard." My response is, "It is just as hard to take care of typical children."

Raising a child with special needs is difficult in different ways. For example, in my situation with my daughter, we have a hard time communicating, as she does not speak. We figure out what she wants and needs based on her expressions, body language (which is also very limited), and the noises she makes throughout the day. However, in other areas, we do not worry as we do with typical children. She doesn't run away in public settings. She does not talk back to us as typical children sometimes do. As each typical child is different, so is each child with special needs different.

For my family and me, some of the most challenging moments are when our daughter has a need and expresses it through crying out and we can't seem to figure out what that need is. For the most part, we can detect this need quickly. Just like a baby, a lot of

191

times we can determine what she needs based on the time of day and the type of cry she makes. If it is lunch or dinner time, she usually wants something to eat. If it is after eating time, her cry usually signals she needs a diaper change. If it is any other time of day, she typically might want attention, music to distract or entertain her, a change in position or scenery, or she simply wants to be held.

However, there are times when we try all of the mentioned things and nothing consoles her. Or when we know she just wants some attention and someone to entertain her, and we can't give it to her then, as there might be other things, children, problems, and so on. We may decide to put off those other problems to help our child with special needs. This depends on how important the problem that we are working on, compared to how uncomfortable or unhappy our child with special needs is. These are some things that become challenging and difficult. However, with the help of respite care and habilitation, some of these moments can be eliminated and that makes things easier to deal with.

Another thing that might be considered challenging with a child with special needs is the amount of time it takes to do things. For example, with our daughter she eats orally and takes two or three times as long sometimes to eat her food. A lot of other kids like her receive nutrition through a tube. That has its own set of challenges, I am sure. For us, we count on it taking a long time when it comes to our daughter and eating. It takes practice for the person feeding her to know how to assist her. Our daughter has a tongue thrust and often spits her food out because she can't control her tongue. She often bites her cheek or tongue too, which may slow things down or make her cry out during feedings.

The things most enjoyable with our daughter are the times she gets in giggly moods and starts laughing. Her smile and laugh are contagious. You can't help but smile and laugh with her. We love to find her tickle spot and make her laugh. It changes the mood in the whole room.

Some of the most precious moments are observing my other children interact with her. We have three younger children and when they give her a hug and a kiss and tell her they love her so sincerely, it melts my heart. I adore watching them play with her. It's a blast when our younger children try to get their older sister to smile or respond in some way. I am also amused when they say something in an altered voice and claim it was our daughter with special needs who said it. She cracks a smile like she understands exactly what is going on.

I love the times when someone tells us about how our daughter with special needs has made an impression on them. For example, one time we got a text from someone at church saying how their daughter loves being in the same class with our daughter. Our friend's daughter enjoys helping our child and seems concerned about her. We've heard several times that our daughter smiles and laughs during singing-time at church. We are told that everyone tries to sing loud to get our daughter to smile or laugh. We are often stopped so someone can say hi to her and she loves the attention. The little things our daughter accomplishes and the kind things people do or say makes a big difference in our lives and our daughter's life.

–A Very Special Child's mother

A year after my interview with this mother of *A Very Special Child*, the father delivered a message to our congregation in church regarding how to gain an understanding of God's plan for us in our lives. When his first daughter was born with health difficulties he had prayed that she would be healed. He felt he had enough faith for that to happen and knew the Lord could heal her. As time passed however, the father came to realize that God's plan for this special child was different from that of her parents. This child with special needs has accomplished spreading more joy to others around her than most of us are capable of in a lifetime. The parents are accepting of the Lord's plan and are thankful for this sweet special child in their family.

Photo provided by the mother

Just in Kason Point Taken

(As told by his mother)

I was 19 and standing in a phone booth (yes, they had those back then) and in the process of updating my sister on my newly single status. It was a nasty breakup of a dysfunctional relationship and in the worked-up state I was in, without thinking, I said, "It's a good thing I'm not pregnant with his kid, cause if I was, I'd abort it!"

Instantly, I was shocked at the words that fell out of my mouth, being as I'd always been pro-life since I first had the thought of forming a stance. The ripple of my words expanded as they reverberated into the universe. Caught up in my drama, I shook off the reprimand my spirit felt for the statement I'd just made.

I worked a day or two at the high-end furniture store where I was employed as a sales associate. On Wednesday, my day off, I scavenged for used furniture to replace the ex-boyfriend's furniture that had left my apartment when he did.

I found some things to make do at the Goodwill shop and arranged to borrow a co-worker's pickup to transport it all home. While driving back to where my purchases were waiting for me, I realized I wouldn't have help moving the large items into my up-stairs apartment. So, I threw out a prayer asking for someone to accommodate.

I arrived curbside. Before I had even closed the door while exit-ing the pickup, a man approached me and asked, "Can I help you?" I laughed and thought, "That was fast, God!" Assuming he worked there, I explained my situation of needing help at my apartment down the road. He agreed to help and turned to secure his bicycle, which, I noticed, had several belongings strapped to it. The sign on the back of his bike read, "Jesus Christ IS Lord. Trust. Believe." My caution radar kicked in and he confirmed when I asked if he worked there, that he did not. But a stronger feeling overrode my caution as I was reminded of my asking for help, here it is. He took on the lifting of each piece of furniture even refusing my help up the stairs. I'm not frail or small so it felt strange that he adamantly refused to let me lift. I dropped him where I'd found him since he said he was waiting on a ride from a friend.

I traded the borrowed pickup for my own car and as I passed the thrift store again, returning home, I noticed him still standing outside. I pulled over and asked him if his ride was coming, and he explained he had missed them while away helping me. I offered him a ride and he accepted as he managed to fit his collapsible bike in my trunk.

Earlier that morning I heard a commercial on the radio for free services at the health department and thought I should get routine testing and rule out the possibility of being pregnant. When I arrived, they were closing for lunch. I was instructed to be back before they closed at four.

Now, ready to drive him wherever he needed, I asked him, "Okay, where to?"

He replied, "Isn't there somewhere you need to be?"

A bit puzzled, I said, "Nooooo, it's my day off, you missed your ride by helping me. I'm happy to take you where you need to go."

He glanced at the clock on my dash and persisted, "Are you sure? It's 3:30 now."

I remembered the health department instructing me to be back before four, but thought, "Oh, I can do that another day, no big deal."

After my hesitation he said, "What did you have planned?"

A bit embarrassed I explained that earlier I went to get a pregnancy test, but they were at lunch and said I could come back before four.

He took me off guard when he asked, matter of factly, "Are you going to keep your baby?"

I laughed nervously, explaining that I wasn't pregnant. I just wanted to rule out the possibility, was all.

He asked me again, "Are you going to keep him? He will be special and evangelise thousands of people."

Either he was crazy or I was. In order to discover which of us was crazy; I headed for the health department with him and proceeded to take the test. While waiting for the results, I wandered outside and found him sitting on a shaded bench with a Bible open on his lap. He beckoned me over and as I sat next to him he pointed to Psalm 139:13-14,

"For thou has possessed my reins: thou hast covered me in my mother's womb. I will praise thee; for I am fearfully and wonderfully made: marvelous are thy works; and that my soul knoweth right well."

Tears fell down my face as I remembered my words spoken in the phone booth days prior. I went back inside where a sweet and cheerful red-headed woman informed me that, indeed, I was expecting.

At 17 weeks along my serum screening came back abnormal, and I was told there was a chance the baby had Down syndrome. After nine ultrasounds, I was told everything looked normal, but they still had concerns about the baby.

On my drive home while listening to a Christian radio station, I was touched by the testimony of a woman, who after receiving an adverse pregnancy diagnosis, decided to go against the doctor's suggestion to abort. Her daughter had been the biggest blessing of her life and as a result, she had written a song titled "Sometimes Miracles Hide".

I felt a prompting to go to the library after praying for the truth of my baby's condition. I had a vision (not abnormal for me as I'd received visions here and there my whole life) of my hand reaching up to remove a book from a shelf. After wandering the library and following my instincts, I found the shelf and removed the book, without looking at the title. I checked it out, face down, and on my way out, turned it over to read its cover: "Expecting Adam—A Story of Birth, Rebirth and Everyday Magic". This book was a true account written by Martha Beck, who had been raised 20 miles from my home-town, about her experiences during pregnancy and of mothering a boy, named Adam, who had Down syndrome.

In April of 2002, my son Kason Jay came into this world via emergency C-section. An hour after I heard his soft cry and he was swept off to the NICU, my midwife timidly informed me he was 4 lbs. 12 oz., and 19 inches long, and appeared to have Down syndrome. I smiled knowingly as she told me I was lucky to have him. She meant that we almost lost him, but I knew the true meaning of being lucky.

He was the sweetest baby, didn't walk until after two, and through many other moments to be mentioned in a much longer story, I gave my heart to the Lord and was made new.

When he was barely five, his needs surpassed my ability to care for him, so he is living in a special needs foster home. While it saddens me that I am not able to provide for and raise him, I take comfort in knowing that a homeless man obeyed God's direction and the world has received someone special.

Kason is 13 years old now, and though I thought I made up his name myself, when he was six months old, I discovered that Kason means: protected by the helmet of salvation.

In case anyone reading this is expecting and facing a decision to take what God has given, my point is we are ALL made, intricately and wonderfully, on purpose. Even if you think you can't do it, there is someone who can and will. Kason is in a loving family with five brothers, each with a special need of his own. There are no disabilities in my opinion, only different abilities. Though he is considered non-verbal, he communicates more effectively than most of us typically developed and his message is so tender and sweet.

-Debbie

Photos provided by Debbie

dis-Abilities

Barbie, now at age 40, says she does not remember having arms. The electrical accident happened when she was only two years of age. Prepare to be amazed at this woman's many accomplishments. There is little she cannot do. She has achieved as much as or perhaps more, than most of us. Meeting with Barbie helped me reflect upon a lot that I take for granted. She has become a motivational speaker, helping others realize their worth, no matter their circumstances.

The youngest of three siblings, Barbie's parents treated her the same way as the rest of her family. She is a Christian and grew up in Texas. Barbie took very personally the bullying she received from children at school, but now realizes that mean children do not target only one child, but usually many.

Being independent meant Barbie had to learn to dress, feed and bathe herself, and yes, with her feet and toes. Her mother encouraged her to keep trying and never give up. Her father also taught her to be self-sufficient. He hoped her fighting spirit would never be crushed.

Going to college at Arizona State University was a huge step for Barbie, which meant moving away from home. She knew she was more than ready to progress with her independence and it helped her to be less introverted. She has always been a self-motivated and independent gal.

At a young age Barbie enjoyed arts and crafts. She learned to swim and roller skate. Today, she continues to enjoy swimming, skating, working out, playing piano and organ, home decorating, karaoke, and shopping. She's even braved skydiving three times and loves it.

From 2002 to 2012, Barbie trained strenuously and followed a strict diet in order to compete in bodybuilding competitions. The other contestants must have felt totally intimidated by this strong woman. She feels relief now at not having such a regimented life.

I set up my meeting with Barbie via text. I pondered, *Wait, how can she text so efficiently and quickly?* She responded to my question without hesitation, "Fast toes? LOL!" Still, I wondered...voice text? Interviewing Barbie was mind-boggling; to hear of the many activities she takes part in. *Unafraid* is the perfect word to describe this woman.

We discussed the rewards and challenges of raising two children. She's had little help, as she's been married and divorced three times. Her first baby was the most difficult to care for. Perseverance was the key to becoming skilled at breast feeding and bathing her little one. She discovered that putting a shirt on her tiny bundle of joy made it easier to give him a bath. Otherwise his squiggly body was way too slippery!

Besides being a mother of her second teenage boy and working as a motivational speaker, Barbie has written a book for children and is currently working on her auto-biography.

If you chance to see Barbie out and about, please don't feel shy about speaking to her. A pet peeve of hers is when people glare at her and then walk right past her without saying a word. Barbie isn't a shy lady. Feel free to talk with her, ask her anything. The question she gets asked most is, "How do you wipe?" You will have to read her upcoming book to find out the answer to this and other important questions.

Interview of Barbie's father, Ben:

I was also fortunate to talk to Barbie's father, Ben, who gave greater insights into how Barbie came to conquer her fears. A retired Houston policeman, Ben is proud that his daughter has reached the potential he always hoped for.

After Barbie's accident, her parents were told that if she lived, she most likely would be a vegetable. Of course, Ben was determined she would survive and become a productive member of society. He wondered, after she healed and learned to live without arms, how would she handle boys and how would boys treat her? His concern was for her emotional and social aspects.

Throughout Barbie's growing up years, Ben thought Barbie would make an excellent personal injury attorney. Considering her driving force, that would have made quite a statement.

As a father, Ben felt protective of Barbie and his other children. When she wanted to skate, he worried she would fall and have nothing with which to catch herself. She could even break her neck! Thankfully, those accidents never happened, and Barbie continues skating to this day.

Another of his concerns was making sure she could swim. He swam along-side Barbie before he allowed her to swim alone. Sometimes Barbie would sneak child-sized floaties on her ankles. This made the upper part of her body dip below the surface. Her father had to put a stop to that!

Ben's hopes for Barbie have been achieved. Since she has accomplished so much on her own, Ben now hopes his daughter will eventually find the right man for her, but take her sweet time doing it. Photos provided by Barbie

A Child's Wisdom

Ryan* related this story of his family to me:

Many years back when my four children were between the ages of five and 11, my wife and I were having a discussion regarding people with special needs. Our youngest, Verna*, was born deaf, and we had all adjusted to her differences in communicating.

Our family had learned a second language, American Sign Language. Verna held her own and was quite independent. If she got mad, closing her eyes was the best way to retaliate. Stomping was another tactic she found to show her unhappiness. Loud volume wasn't an issue for her, but making loud noises herself sure got a rise out of her three siblings attempting to watch television or talk on the phone.

*Names changed to protect privacy

As we were discussing the city's new plans to construct walkways to facilitate wheelchairs, our oldest son, Andrew*, joined the conversation. He told us how sad he felt for handicapped people. We mentioned to him how proud we were that he treated his sister with special needs with equal love and respect. Andrew looked at us with a puzzled expression. He did not know who we were speaking of.

We tried to explain to our oldest son that his youngest sibling was deaf. His reply was, "So?" We found it a bit awkward trying to clarify to him how Verna was really disabled. He argued with us over our explanation. His little sister could do anything and everything. He couldn't understand how we considered her disabled.

This experience gave me hope that Verna would continue to learn and function in society with success. I gained wider prospective on prejudging others. With his pure childlike wisdom, Andrew taught me to focus on capabilities of others instead of their disabilities. Verna is now a productive adult in our society with an independence that surpasses most young adults. It is quite refreshing and rewarding when children teach us valuable lessons.

Gratitude

An acquaintance of mine, who was diagnosed with multiple sclerosis over 40 years ago, describes her life like this:

"People ask me, 'What does MS feel like?' None of us can predict our future, but those of us with multiple sclerosis face endless layers of the unpredictable every waking day."

"MS has become my professor! 'How strange,' you may say. But, I am continuously amazed by the many mini earthquakes that have reorganized my perspective, attitude and reality. Challenges often become or create blessings, depending upon my choice of viewpoint. I love it!"

"I have an imaginary vase that contains my flowers of joy and it overflows. Consequently, I live in a fairly permanent state of gratitude and appreciation. I believe that type of positive energy always generates the same, and the cycle will go on."

-Anonymous

"Healing blessings come in many ways, each suited to our individual needs, as known to Him who loves us best. Sometimes a 'healing' cures our illness or lifts our burden. But sometimes we are 'healed' by being given strength or understanding or patience to bear the burdens placed upon us. ..."[1]

-Dallin H. Oaks

NOTE

1. L.D.S. General Conference October 2006 "He Heals the Heavy Laden"

Proper Perspective

We met Ed at an airport while our flight was delayed four long hours. I believe, perhaps, he, is the reason for our delay. He is an inspiring man, in his mid-30's, born with cerebral palsy, and his parents support him. I look forward to hearing more from him.

Letter from Ed:

I believe everything happens for our highest good, highest growth. Not that life isn't harder than hell, and sometimes you just want to drop a nuke, and break free from this time-trapped realm. Which can be heaven one moment, and hell the next. Yes, it is all in the eye of the beholder. However, I am still figuring out how to focus.

I do not know what life lessons others have learned from my presence in their lives. All I can attest to are the lessons I have learned. One example is patience. Having a physical difficulty speaking the words that are perfectly articulated in my mind makes it hard for most people to see me for who I am. It takes patience and love on my part to interact with the person on the other side of the conversation. This is a side that may have no concept of the reality that I have come to know. Sometimes I come across a reality that I have very little patience for.

Looking back I realize that at a very young age, before I understood, I had an innate understanding that we all live in our own world. That we are all on an individual path. A path to which is anyone's choice. I am still getting lost in trying to figure out where my path leads! For a nickname, my mother called me "Squirrel" when I was little because I would hop around on my knees like a squirrel.

On the personal side of patience, I am still being tested. My patience for myself is quite a bit lower than it is for outside viewers. I believe that is one of the reasons why I chose to experience cerebral palsy during this trip. To strengthen my inner patience.

To date, the biggest lesson I am becoming more aware of is that I am in control! I have a very long way to go before I master this lesson. Yes, I am in control, but in control of what? The summation I have come to grasp is that I am in control of what I focus on. Yes, I have cerebral palsy. Yes, I have many struggles that I live with. I have the control to view them as damned results brought upon me by some outside force. Or, I can view them as stepping stones I deliberately aligned to increase my awareness of an ever-increasing reality.

-Ed

Ed

What a broad outlook Ed's gained in his 30-something years of life. He truly does not let his disability define who he is. I may not ever see this incredible man again, but will never forget "Squirrel".

Airport Luck

I found myself, once again, waiting at an airport longer than planned due to a delayed flight. At least it was only a three-hour wait (cough cough) this time compared to my scheduled departure. Our seat assignments had been changed as well, since it was a smaller plane. This turned out to be for my benefit.

I was seated next to a beautiful Scandinavian woman. Saying hi, I explained how I came to be Nutz. Showing off my Nutz bracelet my husband makes from nuts (not bolts); always make a great ice breaker. In return, I catch their interest as well as a smile. She was a few years younger than me. Conversation led to my interest in people with special needs. My new friend, Esther, has raised one such. Here is her endearing story of her son.

From Matt's mother, Esther:

Being a mother to a child with special needs is exhausting and challenging. In 1984, autism was diagnosed in 1 of 10,000 children (whereas the most current statistics have it now as 1 in 84).

There were no books (and of course, no internet sites) written to assist parents in methods to assimilate their child into an environment which overwhelms their senses. You had to just wing it.

Fortunately, I began attending support group meetings where we shared information and sources to help us integrate our children into society through the medical, educational, and social service agencies. At age seven, Matt was non-verbal himself—but used echolalia to express himself—which no one understood. Auditory training was shown to assist autistic children, talking aloud, so I brought Matt to the Twin Cities for 10 days of this intensive training. Occasionally, Matt could say a word or two, but usually he was so frustrated that I didn't understand his wants and needs that I would also end up in tears—exasperated.

As we were driving home to our rural town five hours away, I was talking and crying to myself (and to God) about how I was unable to handle this complicated, non-verbal child. I felt that I was not capable of raising my son, and that perhaps, he needed to be in a 24-hour facility, as suggested by an outmoded, opinionated pediatrician. I looked at Matt for a moment with my tear-stained face, and he said, "I love you Mom." At that moment, I knew I could do it. I wasn't going to give up, and I certainly was NOT going to hand him over to specialists who felt they knew what was best for my son. In my abyss of self-doubt and hopelessness, I finally understood the profound saying, "Let Go and Let God". From that moment forward, I trusted my intuition to be relentless in securing services and support from positive sources for Matt.

When Matt was around 10 years old, our family moved to Arizona where there were more opportunities for him than in rural Minnesota. My older cousin visited us from South Carolina and spent some time with Matt as I was working full-time. She was the artistic cousin in the family–working in the culinary arts and quite accomplished in painting and drawing, but disillusioned with working in these fields for decades. After becoming involved in Matt's life, she decided to become a special education assistant in the public school system. Within a few years, she obtained her teaching degree and taught her own special education class. It was so inspirational that she would incorporate yoga, music, art, and cooking into her curriculum to provide each student with the opportunity to express themselves in their own individualized manner.

As a parent, we never know if our child's life will inspire others. But Matt affected my cousin, who thereby incorporated her own unique and special abilities to teach other children with special needs to grow and feel good about themselves in a world that otherwise can be hostile and cold.

The journey for the child with special needs in our world is full of apathy and labels. It takes perseverance and dedication as a parent to overcome the negativity that one encounters by society to advocate for your child. That's why I surround myself with encouraging friends, many who are also parents of children with autism.

I remember when Matt was four, a pediatrician told me that he would never talk and to teach him sign language. Some regular education teachers seemed flustered that they had to expend their time to teach Matt assuming he would barely finish high school and would consume time allocated for other students. Psychologists and counselors seemed to reflect an attitude that my parental abilities, or lack of them, contributed to my son's disabilities. A family member discouraged me from having Matt pursue adult skills, such as driving, because he was handicapped. It's as if society wanted me to squirrel him away in a closet. If they don't see him, then they don't have to deal with him.

The labels changed every year, depending on what specialist I visited and what tests they administered. Autistic, autistic-like, schizophrenic, mentally delayed, mentally retarded, Tourette's, Asperger's, attention deficit disorder, obsessive compulsive disorder, and so on. Just pull out the DSM-IV manual and take your pick. (For those of you unfamiliar what it is, the Diagnostic and Statistical Manual of Mental Disorders IV is used by the psychiatric associations to classify your child to determine if they quality for any services). The book is typically considered the bible for any professional who makes psychiatric diagnoses. Through the DSM-IV, clinicians will make a prognosis as to optimal treatment.

Now back to the pediatrician who stated that Matt would never talk. Well, after years of speech and occupational therapy, Matt expresses himself quite eloquently. He completed high school and continued on to community college where he is three courses shy of an associate of arts degree. Through a private driving school, he obtained his driver's license. He shops independently, and weekly, we both attend movies at the theatre, and afterwards, we eat at one of our many favorite restaurants, where waiters know him by name.

Matt has an extensive knowledge of music and movies—what year they were produced, names of actors, songs played and group names, and more. Instead of derogatory comments comparing him to Dustin Hoffman's character in Rain Man with his obsession of dates, perhaps one can put it in perspective that Matt has a photographic memory, and perhaps his ability to categorize information is superior to the average person.

If I hadn't had the opportunity to be included in Matt's journey, I never would have found the wonderful, calming music of Enya, Depeche Mode, and Switchblade Symphony. I never would go individually to the movies to see the Marvel characters, nor would I see movies based on true life personalities like Sully or Snowden. But most importantly, I wouldn't have met the wonderful individuals who helped Matt in his younger days—the volunteer drivers who brought him to speech and physical therapy and horse therapy, or his social worker who helped me obtain a three-wheeler for him to ride, and enrolled him in karate classes, or the speech therapists and the programs that encouraged family involvement.

However, one experience stays with me always. In regular Little League games, the media has shown how parents curse the coaches, the opponent team, and even their own children. There is so much negativity, hostility, stress, and even physical violence, that I cannot believe that it is conducive to positive self-esteem for the young ball players. In the adaptive Little League, parents were always in attendance to cheer EVERY player, whether they had cerebral palsy, Down syndrome, autism, or some other impairment. After every game, parents and children, coaches and friends left with love, respect, appreciation and joy which carried over into their everyday lives.

So enjoy the ride. There will be ups and downs, but ultimately, the reward is that your child will mature into an adult who will amaze you, friends, and family.   *-Esther*

Photos provided by Esther

Champion

When Dan and I observed a young adult jetting around our neighborhood in his electric wheelchair, the thought crossed my mind to ask him for an interview. I shut it down, assuming it would bother him.

Recently, stopping by the house in the middle of the afternoon, which rarely happens on a workday, Dan announced an amusing thing had just happened. He's been driving a non-emergency medical transport van for eight years. The patient he had barely dropped off was the same guy we had seen in the electric wheelchair. Not only that, but he lives directly behind us! We share a common wall and our cats claw vines climb gingerly over to his side of the wall. We have a connection.

Izzy, age 22, was excited to hear about my project. It seems amazing how people are placed in my path for the purpose of spreading awareness to those unfamiliar with such unique individuals. I had thought meeting two such folks at an airport on different occasions was odd enough. But now, all I should have done was practically looked in my own backyard!

Here is an abbreviated life story from our neighbor, Izzy:

When I was born with spina bifida, the doctors told my parents I wouldn't live very long. By the time I turned three, my needs surpassed my mother's ability to care for me. She placed me in a group home where I lived through age 18. I had daily contact with my biological mother all those years. There was a loving couple who cared for me in the group home. I called them my mom and dad. I appreciate them most for being in my life.

When I was 15, I almost died from an awful infection, and I've had many surgeries in my life. At age 17, a doctor attempted to straighten my back by placing two rods in my spine. I suffered with an infection afterwards from May to May, one whole year.

I moved in with my mother and sister two years ago when my group home changed managers. I am in daily contact with my mom and dad from the group home. This was a very difficult move for me, but I know it's for the best.

If I were to describe myself, I'd tell you that I am wheelchair-bound, mostly tube-fed (which is the best for nutritional value), independent, and counselor for a disabled five-year-old boy.

Before I graduated high school at age 18, I played wheelchair basketball and power soccer. You can check it out on You Tube, A.S.U. vs. Arizona Heat power soccer, and see a short clip of me at the beginning. I really miss playing that!

Now, for enjoyment, I play video games, read a lot of Stephan King books, and love watching comedy and action movies, especially the Marvel series.

My most difficult challenge is relationships. I hope to find someone who will care and like me for the person I am. Most people have jumped to conclusions based on my appearance. I need them to give me a chance. I deserve to be treated like any adult desires to be treated.

Recently, someone asked if I could, would I change my circumstances at birth and have the use of my legs. I seriously thought about it for a minute. I decided I am happy with who I am and would not change anything about my life, for it makes me who I am.

My advice to anyone with challenges is to never give up. Don't let anyone talk down to you. Keep trying and do whatever you want to with your life.

-Izzy

There is not anything I could say to add to the above positive outlook on life from this *Champion*! I will be a better person having a backyard connection with Izzy.

Younger photo provided by Izzy

Looking out our backyard into Izzy's

Current

Persistence Pays Off

Being a mother of six, Abby* is never bored. To begin with, having six children is not the norm. What makes this family even more inimitable is child number three has autism. Ray*, the third-oldest child, is now 13 years old.

Through the first year of Ray's life, the only visual sign of his condition was that he didn't present eye contact. This concerned his parents. Abby took her five-month-old baby to a different pediatrician after the first doctor failed to acknowledge her same concerns. Ray's new pediatrician examined the baby's eyes for 10 minutes. At this point (when Ray was eight months old), the doctor did not recognize any problems with his visual acuity, but did with his neurologically processing.

*Names changed to protect privacy

After their move to Connecticut—a state with very progressive testing for children with disabilities—Ray's MRI results showed global delays. Abby had known her baby had autism because of his developmental delays. It was a slight relief to her when Ray was two years old that he was finally diagnosed with autism.

At this time, Ray's father was in medical school, and after much contemplation decided to attain a degree for a Pediatric Geneticist. His colleagues attempted to change his decision. They were perplexed by his choice as the money wasn't any better. It wasn't about the money for Ray's father. He saw a great need in the field.

Genetic testing results in progress each year. Still, 95 percent of tests for genetic defects get no results. With improved testing capabilities, Ray was diagnosed at age six with Microdeletion syndrome. He continues to make strides which amaze the doctors.

"The Savior's teaching that handicaps are not punishment for sin, either in the parents or the handicapped, can also be understood and applied in today's circumstances. How can it possibly be said that an innocent child born with a special problem is being punished? Why should parents who have kept themselves free from social disease, addicting chemicals, and other debilitating substances which might affect their offspring imagine that the birth of a disabled child is some form of divine disapproval? Usually, both the parents and the children are blameless. The Savior of the world reminds us that God 'maketh his sun to rise on the evil and on the good, and sendeth rain on the just and on the unjust.'
(Matt. 5:45.)"[1]

-James E. Faust

NOTE

1.   L.D.S. General Conference October 1984 "The Works of God"

Hold to Life

Life was changed for 32-year-old Ashley when she hit the floor. Coaching the girls' high school freshman basketball team had been a demanding but rewarding job up to this time. A simple accident, being bumped into, and Ashley's life was drastically altered.

There wasn't much Ashley couldn't do before this dreadful day in January of 2016. Her other part-time job was that of a physical therapist. She loved traveling and all sports. She had snowboarded in the French Alps. She enjoyed skateboarding, cycling, football, and soccer, and even had spent a week rafting down the Colorado River in the Grand Canyon. Her life was exhilarating.

At first, Ashley didn't realize the severity of her injury. The day following the accident and while helping a client at physical therapy, she felt a burning, stabbing pain radiate down her leg. This has since left her flat on her back for the majority of her days. Her pain has only increased. Doctors have not been able to address her injury, except with pain medication.

Passing each day lying down in a care facility while staring at four white walls, leaves Ashley depressed. She will soon turn 34 years old and feels more hopeless as times passes on. The world keeps busy outside her window as if nothing were wrong. And yet, time marches on without her.

Attending group therapies and going to various doctor's appointments are practically the only time she gazes upon the outside world, looking up at the sky from her stretcher. People stare as they pass, unwilling to strike up a conversation. Ashley longs for strangers to ask or say something. They only make her feel more out of place, adding to the distress of her situation.

Her body continues to lose the powerful core she once possessed. She has dropped 30 pounds. She feels life being sucked out of her day by day. Journaling does help to pass the dreadfully long hours. Her feelings are dramatic on paper showing much depth, as follows:

"Suffering ebbs and flows purposefully at some point in all our lives, no one is immune. In its wake lies the imprint of those individualized soul lessons that are the impetus for awakening to true Self or backsliding despair, the choice is ours. Buried under masks of perfection and do-ing, in that dark unquenchable chasm, lies our be-ing. I have discovered that attempting to assuage my suffering with worldly clamors only intensified my unendurable pain. This denial of my own soul's innate fervor for completion also denied God's love from dwelling in me. That deep longing for light that we all share is only bestowed through intimate kinship with Love, which is both our origin and destination. Intense suffering compelled my barricade to crumble but it was absolute willingness that enabled the Great Reality to perform a miraculous healing. The way out is not through control, alcohol, or suicide, but rather, through complete surrender into the safe, divine guidance of the all-knowing, loving, powerful Spirit of the Universe."

"The lessons I am accumulating from this incredible experience are indeed perfect. My matter and form coexist in disparate planes. A simple choice to place them in the hands of a true Artist has resulted in the liberation of my soul. My Sculptor is uniting them, despite the broken medium, cleaving frenetic avoidance, chiseling through alcoholism, and polishing my battered soul. I am on the brutal but certain path to becoming my Artist's rendition, the painstaking realization of the realm of dreams."

-Ashley

Photos provided by Ashley

Snowboarding trick

Ashley Rafting Grand Canyon ,   Backpacked Havasupai 26 miles in 1.5 days

Ashley after accident

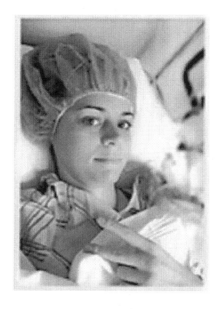

Unwire Me

My Interview with Annette* in her own words:

My son, Michael*, isn't wired the same way as other children. Since he was the third boy of three boys in our family, we knew early on he was exceptional, yet different. He was often not able to sit still or pay attention; he was impulsive; he had emotional out-bursts and got frustrated easily. He never slept well. It hurt me to see that his self-esteem was quite low. Having problems with his speech, Michael had been in speech therapy since the age of three.

Once Michael started school, he slowly fell behind. It was brought to our attention by his teacher when he began kinder-garten that he possibly had an attention issue. I think it is common for parents to live partly in denial. You see and hear the signs, yet part of you tries to move on with life and shut it out in hopes your child will outgrow whatever the problems may be. Our son was young for his grade, and initially we used this as an excuse for his

*Names changed to protect privacy

233

attention difficulties and falling behind. When we started getting notes home from his teacher daily, we decided to visit his pediatrician and bring up some of our concerns, but it wasn't until the end of Michael's kindergarten year.

We received in-depth paperwork to complete. His kindergarten teacher completed the same forms that we did. When we read the results, we were in disbelief. Every single question and answer pointed to severe ADHD. We were at a stand-still at this point. My husband and I were both against medication for ADHD, but we were still on different pages regarding treatment.

Michael attended summer school due to falling behind. Summer came and went and first grade began. The first two weeks were quiet... and then the notes and emails began coming home again. We tried natural supplements to no avail. We visited the pediatrician a few times but never made any concrete decisions. After speaking to fellow parents at my job (I work in a school), we were referred to a counseling center that specialized and did extensive testing for several disorders. Our son spent two hours being tested by the doctor, and a formal written report was provided to us and the school. This was toward the end of first grade, and mind you, Michael was severely behind in reading and writing.

Following testing, Michael had an official ADHD diagnosis and was labeled as a visual learner. The report suggested medication, as the other suggestions we had already implemented (seating him in the front of the class, extra time to organize, and so forth). We attempted to put him on a 504 Plan, but it did not happen. The school said he had made progress since he entered first grade. Knowing what I know now, I would have pushed the 504 Plan more than I did. We, as parents, have the say-so! Demand, demand, demand.

First grade ended. Having to yet again attend summer school, Michael was very upset. Summer came and went again. Second grade started. The teacher received an email from me making her aware of his issues. Michael's first grade teacher gave his second-grade teacher a big file of things that worked for him, and so on.

Testing occurred, showing Michael was far behind his peers in all subjects. His lack of attention and fidgeting, and causing distractions became worse. Our pediatrician suggested trying the lowest possible dose of medication and even breaking it in half. The first day I was quite nervous. I must have checked in that week many times with his teacher. Within the first two days the changes were drastic! Michael sat still. Volunteering with answers surprised his teacher. His sleeping became sound for the first time in years. As Michael made new friends, his confidence boosted. The list goes on and on and on. Michael will tell you he feels better. Going from the messiest student to the most organized student in his class, Michael has amazed us all. The teacher noticed changes. We noticed changes. And most importantly of all, our son noticed changes. We realized we lucked out, as we didn't have to try a different medication as sometimes you do when medicating ADHD. There have not been any ill side-effects and Michael has not failed to thrive (this sometimes can be a side-effect). He takes the medication every single day and will take it during the summer as well. I cannot stress enough what this has done. He went from being behind at the start of the school year and in the low 10th percentile to being in the top 98th percentiles this spring! His speech has improved, and as a matter of fact, he will probably be released from speech therapy during the upcoming school year.

Call it a miracle. Call it whatever you like. What do you have to lose if you are on the fence about medication? Can't hurt to try. You will never know unless you do. Just as people need medication for diabetes, or thyroid disease, to name a few, I feel there is a missing element in the brain for those with ADHD, and medication often replaces what may be lacking. I will remind you, I am not pro-medication. I believe in natural approaches until that proves to not work. Educate yourself. Be an advocate for your kiddo. Utilize your resources; friends, doctors, teachers, online support groups... and never, ever, give up hope. It takes a village!

-Annette

Positive Energy

Grace, a pretty, 14-year-old young lady, born with cerebral palsy, was a delight to interview. She has been blessed with the gift to articulate clearly and her inner beauty radiates.

Having two older and two younger sisters, Grace is sandwiched in the middle. Her father was not home at the time of my interview. I was surrounded by bubbly, fun-loving females and two small dogs slipping frantically across the wood floors as they barked at outside noises. This, to me, was a very average, busy, and loving family.

Grace's mother, Sarah, mentioned how differently most strangers view her child in a wheelchair. One occasion when Grace was four years old, Sarah was pushing her daughter's wheelchair at a nearby mall. Sarah's sister was pushing her own child in a stroller. They switched wheelchair for stroller, as Sarah was curious to see her sister's reaction as people walked by. After a few minutes, her sister had gained an understanding of what Sarah had seen from people passing by. They would either stare or ignore the child in the wheelchair. However, the child seated in the stroller was smiled at, talked to, or even given a physical touch from on-lookers.

Having a desire to know Grace, I asked her a few generic questions to begin with; her answers show how very typical she is:

Favorites: Color—dark blue; food—Mexican food (Taco Bell); dessert—vanilla ice cream with peanut butter swirled through it, the way her father makes it—yum; television show—the cartoon, "My Little Pony Friendship is Magic"; music—pop (lots of songs); having fun with friends; and playing games on the Nintendo Wii.

One of the best fictional but realistic books Grace ever read is titled "Wonder". It's a story about a boy who was born with a dis-figured face. It shows that when he opened up to people, they be-gan to appreciate what was on the inside. They stopped thinking about his appearance.

Grace thought of two favorite movies. One is *Never Ending Story*. Another is *Divergent*. She enjoyed how this movie smoothly transitioned into many different perspectives.

Grace takes the most pleasure at school when she's laughing with her friends. She stated how fun it is to be with them giggling hysterically at random things. Another thing Grace especially looks forward to is when she has no homework. The academic class she learns the most in is Social Studies. Her brilliant mind holds on to historical facts, which she finds very interesting.

When asked about her dislikes about school she quickly responded, "Homework and long essays that have to be in a certain format." In many aspects, Grace seems very typical for a young teenage girl.

One of Grace's pet peeves is to be treated like a baby. An example of that is when someone continually asks her to give *five*. It annoys her also when they use baby talk, as if she can't understand ordinary English.

Grace belongs to a group called The East Valley Millennial Choir. They perform with a symphony orchestra at The Mesa Arts Center in Mesa, Arizona. Musical numbers include classical and operatic pieces.

Three years ago, Grace met a friend who was very shy. After Grace talked with this girl often, they became very close pals. They aren't as close now, since Grace has second lunch at school, while her friend has first lunch.

Some hopes that Grace has for her life include becoming a writer. She's learning to write her biography and post it on the internet under "Watt's Pad". The career that Grace may choose is computer animation. After she gets married she'd like to have mostly girls and one boy. Grace loves to spin herself in her wheelchair. Her husband would need to spin her often!

This 45-minute discussion with young Grace gave me a better grasp on the strength it takes to live life to the fullest when given overwhelming physical challenges. Her courage and optimism surpasses most.

Photo provided by Sara

Grace

6

Conclusion-
Metamorphosis

There are four stages in the metamorphosis of butterflies and moths: egg, larva, pupa, and adult. Butterflies, moths, beetles, flies and bees have complete metamorphosis. [1]

My theory regarding people with special needs and disabilities is similar to the butterfly metamorphosis. Most of us trip upon uneven pebbles in life and experience our ongoing metamorphosis. Some manage accomplishments toward this change with ease, but others feel their pebbles are an unending mountainous range with jagged ridges. Assessing clients' struggles from day to day, I've acquired thankfulness for the jagged ridges of my trials.

Those born with special needs/disabilities and others who become so through accidents, illness, or disease obtain metamorphosis at a much slower rate. Onlookers may not see hope or the slightest chance of success and joy for this unique group of individuals. Much is left unseen by the naked eye.

I do not claim to understand the full plan of our Creator. I know He has the greatest love for all His children. I feel those with the most noticeable differences are His most beautiful creation. It is unknown when they will complete their metamorphosis. This happening could be God's most lovely and spectacular project. They will become His Monarch Butterflies.

NOTE

1. http://www.ansp.org/explore/online-exhibits/butterflies/lifecycle/

7

Epilogue

This last year was exceptionally dramatic for the lives of several of my clients and their families. Many changes have taken place. Some things were planned and others were a surprise.

With the passing of Lloyd (*Not Twins, Heavenly Laughter*), and David (*No Difference*), I have felt the loss of them. Although Lloyd and David never spoke a word, there was communication given to those who paid attention to them. These unique and brave individuals left a bright mark in the Nutz household.

A few months before I concluded this project, two families have completed major living arrangement changes for their children with special needs. With ongoing and worsening medical conditions, these parents have taken the utmost care in providing the best environment with loving care and comfort for their children. Amazingly, a group home was found where all four of the quadruplets (*Life x 4)* could reside which was in their best interest.

Three weeks later, I was told by Aurelia's mother (*Not Twins*) that, because of Aurelia's recent serious medical setbacks, they were searching for the best group home to place her in. With all the many choices of group homes in the area, only those who've gone through this experience can relate to what an immense task this is.

After Aurelia was moved into the group home which best catered to her needs, her mother sent me a text to let me know that there are quadruplets (*Life x 4*) at Aurelia's new temporary residence. These two families have never met and do not know each other. Visiting these five special friends has been made easier. I had a heart full of gratitude knowing this was not a coincidence.

"...this was all part of God's 'divine design.' We all have similar things happen in our lives. We may meet someone who seems familiar; renew an acquaintance; or find common ground with a stranger."[1]

-Ronald A. Rasband

Note

1.   L.D.S. General Conference September 30, 2017 "By Divine Design"

<u>8.</u> Definitions

ambulatory: Able to walk about; not bedridden.

anxiety (medical): An abnormal and overwhelming sense of apprehension and fear often marked by physical signs (such as tension, sweating, and increased pulse rate), by doubt concerning the reality and nature of the threat, and by self-doubt about one's capacity to cope with it, mentally distressing concern or interest.

Asperger syndrome: Delays in development of many basic skills, such as ability to socialize and communicate with others and use imagination. Individuals usually have normal intelligence and near-normal language development.

atrophy: Gradual decline in effectiveness or vigor due to under use or neglect.

attention-deficit/hyperactivity disorder (ADHD): A brain disorder marked by an ongoing pattern of inattention and/or hyperactivity or impulsivity that interferes with functioning or development.

autism: Serious neurological developmental disorder that impairs a child's ability to communicate and interact with others.

cerebral palsy: A neurological disorder caused by a non-progressive brain injury or malformation that occurs while the child's brain is under development. It primarily affects body movement and muscle coordination.

Down syndrome: Most common genetic chromosomal disorder and cause of learning disabilities in children. Genetic disorder caused when abnormal cell division results in extra genetic material from chromosome 21.

echolalia: The immediate and involuntary repetition of words or phrases just spoken by others, often a symptom of autism.

emotional disability: Emotional or behavioral disability that impacts a person's ability to effectively recognize, interpret, control, and express fundamental emotions. The Individuals with Disabilities Education Act of 2004 characterizes the group of disabilities as Emotional Disturbance (ED).

executive function: A set of mental skills that help you get things done. These skills are controlled by an area of the brain called the frontal lobe.

eye-hand coordination: The coordinated control of eye movement with hand movement, and the processing of visual input to guide reaching and grasping along with the use of proprioception of the hands to guide the eyes.

failure to thrive (FTT): More recently known as faltering weight or weight faltering, is a term used in pediatric and adult medicine, as well, to indicate insufficient weight gain or inappropriate weight loss. When not more precisely defined, the term refers to pediatric patients.

farsighted: Seeing objects at a distance more clearly than those near at hand.

504 Plan: A plan developed to ensure that a child who has a disability identified under the law and is attending an elementary or secondary educational institution receives accommodations that will ensure their academic success and access to the learning environment.

gastrostomy feeding tube (G-tube): A special tube in the stomach to deliver food and medication for patients unable to chew or swallow. Sometimes it is replaced by a button, called a Bard Button or Mic-Key.

glaucoma: An eye disease with certain features including an intraocular pressure that is too high for the continued health of the eye.

grand mal seizure: A seizure marked by abrupt loss of consciousness with initially prolonged tonic muscle contractions followed by clonic muscle spasms.

group home: A home where a small number of unrelated people in need of care, support, or supervision can live together, such as those who are elderly, physically, or mentally ill.

IEP: The Individualized Educational Plan is a plan or program developed to ensure that a child who has a disability identified under the law and is attending an elementary or secondary educational institution receives specialized instruction and related services.

leukemia: A malignant progressive disease in which the bone marrow and other blood-forming organs produce increased numbers of immature or abnormal leukocytes. These suppress the production of normal blood cells, leading to anemia and other systems.

lupus: A chronic inflammatory disease that occurs when your body's immune system attacks your own tissues and organs. Inflammation caused by lupus can affect many different body systems—including your joints, skin, kidneys, blood cells, brain, heart and lungs.

meningomyelocele: Protrusion of the membranes that cover the spine but some of the spinal cord itself through a defect in the bony encasement of the vertebral column. The bony defect is spina bifida.

mental retardation: Sub average intellectual ability equivalent to or less than an IQ of 70 that is accompanied by significant deficits in abilities (as in communication or self-care) necessary for independent daily functioning, is present from birth or infancy, and is manifested especially by delayed or abnormal development by, learning difficulties, and by problems in social adjustment.

Microdeletion syndrome: Syndrome caused by a chromosomal deletion smaller than 5 million base pairs (5 Mb) spanning several genes that is too small to be detected.

mosaic: A person or a tissue that contains two or more types of genetically different cells. All females are mosaics because of X-chromosome inactivation (lyonization). Mosaic patterns can affect the way genetic disorders are expressed.

multiple sclerosis: Also known as MS, is a chronic disease that attacks the central nervous system, i.e. the brain, spinal cord and optic nerves. In severe cases, the patient becomes paralyzed or blind while in milder cases there may be numbness in the limbs.

obsessive compulsive disorder (OCD): A mental health disorder that affects people of all ages and walks of life, and occurs when a person gets caught in a cycle of obsessions and compulsions. Obsessions are unwanted, intrusive thoughts, images or urges that trigger intensely distressing feelings.

Pediatric Geneticist: A doctor with special training in pediatrics and genetics. They are able to recognize rare genetic syndromes and conditions in children and help families of children with these conditions to receive appropriate medical care.

proprioception: Relating to stimuli that are produced and perceived within an organism, especially those connected with the position and movement of the body.

respite: Providing or being in temporary care to relieve a primary caregiver.

ring 18: A genetic condition caused by a deletion of the two tips of chromosome 18 followed by the formation of a ring-shaped chromosome. It was first reported in 1964.

sensory: Of or relating to sensation, or physical senses; transmitted or perceived by the senses.

schizencephaly: (from Greek skhizein, meaning to 'split', and encephalon, meaning 'brain') is a rare birth defect characterized by abnormal clefts lined with grey matter that form the ependyma of the cerebral ventricles to the pia mater. These clefts can occur bilaterally or unilaterally. Common clinical features of this malformation include epilepsy, motor deficits, and psychomotor retardation.

schizophrenia: A mental disorder that is characterized by disturbances in thought (such as delusions), perception (such as hallucinations), and behavior (such as disorganized speech or catatonic behavior), by a loss of emotional responsiveness and extreme apathy, and by noticeable deterioration in the level of functioning in everyday life.

scoliosis: An abnormal curving of the spine.

special needs: Mental, emotional or physical problems in a child that requires a special setting for education.

spina bifida: A major birth defect and a type of neural tube defect that involves an opening in the vertebral column caused by the failure of the neural tube to close properly during embryonic development. (The neural tube is the structure in the developing embryo that gives rise to the brain and spinal cord.) Because of the defect in the spine, part of the spinal cord is exposed and protrudes as a meningomyelocele.

Tourette syndrome (TS or simply Tourette's): A common neuropsychiatric disorder with onset in childhood, characterized by multiple motor tics and at least one vocal (phonic) tic. These tics characteristically wax and wane, can be suppressed temporarily, and are typically preceded by an unwanted urge or sensation in the affected muscles. Some common tics are eye blinking, coughing, throat clearing, sniffing, and facial movements. Tourette's does not adversely affect intelligence or life expectancy.

 tracheostomy: A surgical procedure which consists of making an incision on the anterior aspect of the neck and opening a direct airway through an incision in the trachea (windpipe). The resulting stoma (hole), or tracheostomy, can serve independently as an airway or as a site for a tracheal tube or tracheostomy tube to be inserted; this tube allows a person to breathe without the use of the nose or mouth.

tube feeding: A flexible tube passed into the stomach for introducing fluids and liquid food. For patients who are unable to swallow safely. This medical treatment is used in acute conditions or lifelong chronic disabilities.

9. Reader's Reviews

*"I knew the author when we were in high school, but I had no idea that she had dedicated her life to these exceptional members of our society. **Look IN Me** shares so much to which we all need to be exposed. Her tales of her experiences with the physically and/or mentally handicapped touched me deeply I could feel the joy and humor of her life in every word. I enjoyed her stories so much, through the difficulties and sometimes even sadness. This book opens up a world that most people are never exposed to in their lifetimes. Please read and share this book."*

-Linda Holder, retired Librarian

"This book opened my eyes, my mind and — most of all — my heart. People I might hardly have noticed in the past jump into my awareness in full 3-D." *-Jeff McCollum*

*"**Look IN Me** is a wonderful book written by one of the most compassionate people I know. I call Diane an angel. She has provided love and care to many children and adults with special needs. This book is a treasure chest full of her experiences over the years, as well as interviews of those with disabilities. Some of her stories will make you laugh, and some will make you cry, but they will always touch your heart and teach a lesson about life, love, and caring. I loved reading this book!"* *-L. Signor*

Made in the USA
San Bernardino, CA
31 July 2018